TEEN PREGNANCY CHALLENGE

Book One

Also by Jeanne Lindsay and Sharon Rodine:

Teen Pregnancy Challenge, Book Two: Programs for Kids

By Jeanne Lindsay and Catherine Monserrat:

*Adoption Awareness: Help for Teachers,
Counselors, Nurses and Caring Others*

By Jeanne Warren Lindsay:

*Teens Parenting: The Challenge of Babies and Toddlers
Do I Have a Daddy? A Story About a Single-Parent Child
Teenage Marriage: Coping with Reality
Teens Look at Marriage: Rainbows, Roles and Reality
Parents, Pregnant Teens and the Adoption Option:
Help for Families
Pregnant Too Soon: Adoption Is an Option
Open Adoption: A Caring Option*

TEEN PREGNANCY CHALLENGE

CHALLENGE

Book One
Strategies for Change

Jeanne Warren Lindsay, M.A., C.H.E.

and

Sharon Rodine, M.Ed.

Morning
Glory
Press

Buena Park, California

Library of Congress Cataloging-in-Publication Data

Lindsay, Jeanne Warren.
    Teen pregnancy challenge.

    Includes bibliographical references.
    Contents: v. 1. Strategies for change --
v. 2. Programs for kids.
    1. Teenage mothers--United States. 2. Teenage pregnancy--
United States. 3. Social work with teenagers--United States.
I. Rodine, Sharon.   II. Title.
    HQ759.4.L559 1989   362.7'96   89-14491
    ISBN 0-930934-41-5 (set)
    ISBN 0-930934-40-7 (set : pbk.)
    ISBN 0-930934-35-0 (v. 1)
    ISBN 0-930934-34-2 (v. 1 : pbk.)
    ISBN 0-930934-39-3 (v. 2)
    ISBN 0-930934-38-5 (v. 2 : pbk.)

MORNING GLORY PRESS, INC.
6595 San Haroldo Way   Buena Park, CA 90620
Telephone (714) 828-1998
Printed and bound in the United States of America

To the NOAPP Board Members,
past and present,
whose vision has created a national network
of support for young people
and whose dedication and commitment
continues to change lives.

Morning Glory Press, Inc.
is pleased to publish

Teen Pregnancy Challenge, Book One and *Book Two*

in cooperation with

The National Organization on Adolescent Pregnancy
and Parenting, Inc. (NOAPP)

NOAPP is a national membership network dedicated
to preventing adolescent pregnancy
and problems related to adolescent sexuality,
pregnancy and parenting.

To join NOAPP, or for information, contact
Executive Director
NOAPP
P.O. Box 2365
Reston, VA 22090
703/435-3948

Contents

PUTTING GUIDELINES INTO PRACTICE   195

By Betty Dodson
El Paso, Texas—Project Redirection, Meeting a
community's needs; Comprehensive services offered;
Recruit school dropouts; Staffing and case management; Education services; Health care coordinated; Use
of volunteers; Day care homes augment school centers;
Emergency housing available; Transportation system
inadequate; Therapeutic counseling provided; Teen
father involvement; Family center; Prevention
component; Success stories.

Preface

That a considerable number of young people are in serious trouble throughout the United States is well documented. Once school teachers thought the worst discipline problems among adolescents were gum chewing, profanity, and defacement of property. We now find young people involved deeply with drugs and alcohol, early sexual activity, and childbearing. Teens are dropping out of school at a great rate and consigning themselves to a non-productive future.

Of all the issues of adolescent failure syndrome, one of the most devastating is too-early childbearing and childrearing. This impacts not only the greatest numbers of people, but also the generations-at-risk being produced.

According to the recent report released by the National Research Council of the National Academy of Sciences, *Risking the Future* , (p. 1) "Regardless of one's political philosophy or moral perspective, the basic facts are disturbing: more than one million teenage girls in the United States become pregnant each

year, just over 400,000 teenagers obtain abortions, and nearly
470,000 give birth."

Our society cannot afford to ignore the negative impact on
both young women and young men that untimely parenting has
on their education and the related limitation of career opportunities. Neither can society afford to ignore the babies, many of
them high-risk, born to teen mothers each year.

Prevention of too-early pregnancy is a complex and difficult
goal. Whoever and wherever we are, we can work toward this
goal. Children who feel a connectedness with their families and
their community, who enjoy and do well in school, who receive
the health and social services they need, are less likely to
become pregnant too soon or to cause an unintended pregnancy.

For those teens who do become parents before they're ready
to handle this responsibility independently, carefully designed
and implemented services can help them avoid some of the
negative consequences so often faced by teenage parents.

Teen Pregnancy Challenge, Book One: Strategies for Change
provides guidelines for people concerned about this challenge,
guidelines for developing adolescent pregnancy prevention and
care programs.

Its companion volume, *Teen Pregnancy Challenge, Book
Two: Programs for Kids* focuses more directly on established
programs providing services along the prevention continuum
from primary prevention to support services for teenage parents.

Foreword

As I travel around the country, it is readily apparent that more than ever young people need mentors and advocates. They need us to create the conditions that help them make positive choices about the rest of their lives.

In today's high tech society, most teenagers are well advised to postpone parenthood into their twenties, or even later. What makes teenage parenthood a more critical issue than it was in the days of our coming-of-age is not so much the number and the rate of pregnancies and births as it is the severity of the price paid for too-early childbearing.

It's not just a personal issue. Although teenage mothers or fathers face some very bleak prospects, their children's future is also at risk. A very large proportion of teenage families will never be able to achieve anything close to the standard of living that the average American family once took for granted.

Given the competitive market place, an education is the key to getting a job that pays decent wages. According to the

Children's Defense Fund, since the 1960s the earning power of high school dropouts has fallen twenty-two percent in relation to the earning power of graduates.

It is harder and harder to get a permanent job with a promising future for someone who hasn't finished college, much less high school. Yet only six out of ten teenage mothers will have a high school diploma, compared with nine in ten of their peers who delayed parenthood. A disproportionate number of young fathers drop out of school as well, which means that becoming a parent too soon is not simply a temporary disruption in a teen's life. It often means a long-term—and losing—struggle against the chill winds of poverty, or near-poverty.

In stark contrast to society's ideal of marriage and family life, many teen mothers raise their children without the help of the children's fathers. The decline in the marriage rate among teenagers is due in part to the fact that median earnings of young men have fallen substantially since the early 1970s. Apparently, males earning low wages are far less likely to marry than their peers with higher earnings.

For whatever the reasons, marriage rates among all teens, including pregnant teens and teenage mothers, have tumbled; more than four out of five mothers under age twenty will be unmarried in the next decade if present trends continue.

This doesn't bide well for the children born to these young women. Because the wages of young workers have dropped significantly since 1973, two incomes are increasingly necessary to maintain a family above the poverty line. The inadequate education and low wages of young parents, combined with the fact that teenage mothers are more likely to be unmarried, means that the vast majority of children of teenagers are, or will be, poor.

Although it seems, at least at first glance, that decreasing teenage parenthood is basically a matter of preventing teenage pregnancy, a second look reveals that teenage pregnancy is a symptom, not a cause. There is an established relationship between poverty, limited schooling and life options, and early parenthood.

Although teen pregnancy and parenthood crosses all boundaries—rich and poor; black, Hispanic, and non-Hispanic white; urban and rural communities—disadvantaged teens are more likely to fall into the trap of too-early childbearing. About one of every five teenagers, ages sixteen to nineteen, with below-average basic academic skills and from families with incomes below the poverty level, is a parent. In contrast, only about one out of every twenty teens in the same age group who have average or better skills and family incomes above the poverty level is a parent, regardless of race or ethnicity.

Although most agree that being an adolescent parent is not in the young person's best interest, there are many different—and often conflicting—views about what to do about it. It's time to put these differences aside and focus on how to achieve our shared goals: motivating young people to reach their own full potential and ensuring that they are able to take advantage of the opportunities our society provides.

No matter our own personal beliefs about teenage sexuality, teens won't hear moralizing lectures (just as we didn't). Clearly, we can't wait for young people to come to us for help. We must reach out to them.

This book couldn't be more welcomed. It is a concise, complete guide on how to help young people "beat the odds" for becoming a teenage parent and, at the same time, it offers solid advice on what can be done to help teenage parents avoid the negative consequences of too-early parenthood.

It identifies promising new approaches as well as proven strategies for the planning, delivering, and monitoring of a variety of programs. Moreover, it offers unique insight: slice-of-life "snapshots" of young people's thoughts, and of their lives, to give us a clear picture of what teens think about and what their lives are like.

Don't be overwhelmed by the vast numbers and problems linked to teenage parenthood. It is a challenge to make a dent in those statistics, but one that can be tackled.

First of all, we can peel away the superficial characteristics society gives to "teenagers" and look for the young individuals struggling to find themselves and their place in a world of other people. You neither have to be an expert about community development to work with young people nor hip to the latest nuances of teenage culture to relate to them. Your own life experience and your own interest in them goes a long way.

You can make a difference: note the variety of programs and resources described in this book alone.

You don't have to reach all the teenagers in your community. Just touching the lives of two or three young people is a positive step in the right direction.

Carol Cassell, Ph.D., Author and Lecturer
Straight from the Heart: How to Talk to Your Teenagers About Love and Sex. 1987: Simon and Schuster.
Sexuality Education: A Resource Book. 1989: Garland Press. Edited with Pamela Wilson.
Swept Away: Why Women Fear Their Sexuality. 1984: Simon and Schuster.

Acknowledgments

We especially appreciate the many program providers who shared their experiences with us as we worked on this book and its partner, *Teen Pregnancy Challenge, Book Two: Programs for Kids*. We quote a lot of them in the following chapters, and have included their program names, addresses, and telephone numbers in the Appendix, pages 217-228. These Appendix pages are simply an extension of our Acknowledgments.

People quoted in *Book Two* are listed in the Appendix of that volume.

We've also talked with and interviewed teens including young fathers and mothers. Their sharing has touched us deeply.

During the first stages of *Teen Pregnancy Challenge,* Ellen Peach helped conceptualize its direction. She also helped edit the final manuscript. Other NOAPP board members who read and commented on the manuscript include Mary Ann Liebert, Sue Dolezal, Marie Mitchell, Lois Gatchell, Caroline Gaston, and Barbara Huberman. Every board member, in fact, contributed to these books. This is truly a joint project.

Genie Wheeler of Pathfinder Publishing, Pat Alviso, and Erin Lindsay also helped us with editing. Our husbands, Dick Rodine and Bob Lindsay, edited, listened, challenged, and encouraged us, and were amazingly supportive of our immersion in our project for many weeks. Brent and Michael Rodine are delighted the books are finished.

Tim Rinker designed the covers and Steve Lindsay helped with book design. Erin Lindsay prepared the charts. Carole Blum spent many hours proofreading, encouraging, and tolerating.

We appreciate them all.

We also thank each other. We've worked together on many issues of the *NOAPP Network,* but never quite as hard as we've worked on *Teen Pregnancy Challenge, Book One* and *Book Two.* It's been hard labor . . . but a labor of love.

Jeanne Lindsay
Sharon Rodine
July, 1989

Introduction

Increasingly, local communities are recognizing the serious-
ness of the teen pregnancy challenge. Because the causes of teen
pregnancy and parenting are complex, approaches to solutions
are varied. The most effective programs exist when caring
individuals and agencies combine their resources and energies in
a cooperative, comprehensive approach to serve young people
and their families. This is happening in many communities
today, and it is making a difference in the lives of young people.

NOAPP Focus Is on Teen Pregnancy

The National Organization on Adolescent Pregnancy and
Parenting, Inc. (NOAPP) is a membership organization of
service providers and community leaders at the local and state
level who work diligently to prevent too-early childbearing.
NOAPP's aim, when too-early pregnancy occurs, is to prevent
the negative consequences of early childbearing by providing
appropriate intervention services to pregnant and parenting teens

and their families. NOAPP board members direct many
successful programs and are leaders in this field.

Through identification and involvement of service providers,
NOAPP is able to set up channels of communication for the
sharing of ideas and resources. Many states have statewide
organizations addressing teen pregnancy issues. In other states,
NOAPP has identified key agencies and individuals who provide
leadership on the subject at the local level. Names, addresses,
and phone numbers of these state contacts are listed in the
Appendix of *Teen Pregnancy Challenge, Book 2: Programs for
Kids*.

By answering requests for help and by assisting with conferences and training events around the nation, NOAPP has become aware of the many existing models for human services.
This experience has underscored the fact that there is no one
right way to organize services for troubled teens . . . there is no
quick fix or magic solution. Each community must decide what
works best for its own situation. The one common denominator
is that somehow the physical and mental health, education, and
social service resources must be brought together in a systematic
service delivery system over a several-year time span to make a
significant difference in the lives of teenagers, their families,
and their offspring.

As NOAPP's executive director (Sharon Rodine) and newsletter editor (Jeanne Lindsay), we have collected information on
hundreds of adolescent pregnancy programs providing prevention or care intervention services at the local community level.
We interviewed in depth many people involved in providing
these services, and talked with and/or received written
information from several hundred others.

These program providers shared their successes and their
failures with us, their dreams for these young people who need
assistance to develop healthy, happy, and successful futures for
themselves. They told us why they are involved with young
people, what they hope to accomplish, and of the tremendous
need for community-wide support for these programs.

They spoke often of the power of parental involvement, and
of the expressed needs of many parents as they struggle to help

their children cope with the pressures of our sexually permissive society.

The programs represent a diversity of settings, community sizes, geographic locations, target populations, and operational structures and methods. The focus goes beyond looking at the factors involved in creating and sustaining a program that meets the identified community need. The information also addresses the less concrete but equally important intangible factors that are critical in creating a program which radiates a caring, nurturing feeling for the young people being served.

Scope of *Teen Pregnancy Challenge*

Defining the scope of *Teen Pregnancy Challenge, Book One* and *Book Two* was difficult. A great deal of research on teen pregnancy issues has been completed, and more is currently in progress. Numerous documents have been published reporting on the results of the research.

Several states have published well-edited reports on teen pregnancy in their regions. Some of these publications include excellent bibliographies. Other publications contain directories of teen pregnancy prevention and care programs within specific states or across the country.

There are resources which focus on abstinence or on contraceptive teaching. Some authors concentrate on describing programs or methods of providing prenatal care, parenting support, and/or child care for adolescent parents. The responsibilities of the schools in providing education and job development services for young people including teen parents is another topic recently covered in several publications. See the *Teen Pregnancy Challenge* Appendixes for a listing of many of these materials.

We had no intention of duplicating these admirable efforts. Our aim is simply to provide practical, down-to-earth guidance to those interested in developing adolescent pregnancy prevention and care services.

Teen Pregnancy Challenge, Book One: Strategies for Change describes generically how to develop services. It provides specific step-by-step guidelines for developing programs to help

young people, whether those programs are designed to help
parents of preschoolers talk about sexuality with their children,
encourage teens to delay sexual intercourse, provide birth
control counseling and services to sexually active young people,
and/or offer the comprehensive services needed by teens already
pregnant or parenting.

How to document the need for any—or all—of these services
is explained. The importance of and strategies for building
community support are addressed. Tips are given for planning a
program, designing the content, and choosing the setting. A
chapter is devoted to the search for funding, another to evaluation techniques. Marketing strategies presented include outreach to potential clients, public relations within the community,
and advocacy on the local, state and national levels.

Examples of diverse local community programs are included
to illustrate the concepts presented. We hope these examples
may inspire other communities to expand their program vision
and to enhance their service approaches. Contact names, addresses, and telephone numbers for most of the programs
mentioned in the following chapters are included in the Appendix. The Appendix also includes a list of resource organizations
to contact for further information and technical assistance.

Book Two Features Programs for Kids

Teen Pregnancy Challenge, Book Two: Programs for Kids
focuses even more directly on local programs along the prevention continuum from primary prevention through parenting
support. Featured are programs from a wide variety of settings—
schools, churches, health clinics, agricultural extension service,
4-H, Urban League, and others.

The book is far more than a catalog or a directory of services   ·
listing names, addresses, contact persons, goals, objectives, and
numbers served. Instead, the program directors speak for themselves, people who, sometimes against great odds, are helping
young people gain self-esteem, set personal goals, and achieve
those goals instead of having a baby too soon.

They talk about their difficulties in convincing their
organizations and communities of the need to get involved in

teen pregnancy prevention, of their search for funding, and their strategies for building community support. They discuss the needs of their clients, young people who face daily the sexual messages of our time. They share their ideas for creating programs that help young people grow into responsible, caring, self-sufficient adults.

The adolescent pregnancy prevention continuum governs the organization of *Teen Pregnancy Challenge, Book Two: Programs for Kids*.

After a discussion of the unique aspects of adolescence, various programs are described across the country which are helping youth prevent too-early pregnancy, programs in the schools and throughout the community. People in these prevention programs discuss how they help young people learn the assertive techniques they need to remain sexually abstinent in a world that screams "Do it" from billboards and TV screens across the country.

Prevention doesn't stop, however, at the delaying-sexual-intercourse spot on the continuum. One chapter suggests approaches for working with sexually active youth, another with pregnancy alternatives counseling. People in these programs discuss the need for providing contraceptive information and methods for young people already sexually active, and of strategies for helping youth understand the tremendous responsibilities which accompany sexual intercourse.

Males are the focus of one chapter, with described programs ranging from sexuality education for little boys to group support, job training, and employment help for young fathers.

The prevention continuum extends to programs focusing on pregnant adolescents, the time to prevent health problems for the young mothers and for their babies. Providing services for the many needs of teen parents helps prevent the adverse effects so often associated with adolescent parenting.

Child care programs are an integral part of the prevention continuum, and not only because access to child care allows the teen mother to continue her education. Good child care also gives the children a positive start in life, especially if the parents are helped to improve their parenting skills.

Contact NOAPP for More Information

We could not include all the agencies and programs NOAPP contacted in gathering information for these books. A vast amount of additional care and prevention program information is included in NOAPP's resource files, and is available upon request.

Mary Ann Liebert, NOAPP president, states, "If the problem of adolescent pregnancy is to be addressed effectively at all, it can best be addressed at the local level. What young people most need are adults who care enough about them to invest their time and attention in that young person's life and with that young person's needs."

In effect, these books become more than handbooks of ideas. They salute all program professionals and community leaders who not only care about today's youth and for generations to come, but are also actively involved in inventing a better future for these young people.

Serving our nation's future is everybody's obligation. Being models of caring, responsibility, and self-respect begins with the ME in each of us. A self-examination of these qualities is our first step. The second step is to help young people be self-respecting, caring, responsible individuals.

These books are written for those who have taken, or who will soon take, that second step.

CHAPTER **1**

Our Children— Our Future

Remember when only "those girls" got pregnant? In the not so distant past, we thought "nice girls didn't." If a nice girl did, she was expected to marry the father quickly, and seven months later she'd deliver an eight-pound "preemie."

The literature of the 1950s suggests psychological problems caused teenagers to conceive. Seldom was a partner mentioned. According to the theory of the time, perhaps "unwed" and pregnant teenagers needed help, but they certainly should not be mixed up with "regular" kids.

In fact, when California legislators allocated money for special school programs for pregnant minors in 1967, they specified the programs could not be located on school campuses. Were they suggesting pregnancy was contagious?

We're fully aware now, of course, that living in a lovely home with an all-American family does not always protect a young woman from too-early pregnancy or a young man from fathering a child before he's ready to parent. Teen pregnancy

cuts across all ethnic and socio-economic lines, and hits all
communities.

Too-early pregnancy changes lives within our communities,
and the outcome may be disastrous. Not only is the young
woman affected, but also her partner, their families, and especially their child. Marriage is not likely to solve those problems.

The results—school dropout, dependence on welfare, children without fathers, pain for the extended family members,
young parents without a future, spousal abuse, and children
at risk.

Intervention can make a difference. The best intervention is
early enough to prevent the untimely pregnancy. For those teens
already pregnant, intervention can often prevent the school
dropout, dependence on welfare, and children-at-risk. Sherry
demonstates the results of comprehensive intervention. Her story
is real, as are the other vignettes and quotes from young people
included in this book.

Sherry's Story

Sherry, 17, the attractive blue-eyed blonde mother of one-
year-old Sammy, is close to high school graduation. She works
every afternoon as a file clerk for a local attorney. Without the
help of her special school, she says she would have dropped out
long ago.

Sherry's parents live in an upper-middle class neighborhood
in Albuquerque, New Mexico. Her father is sales manager for a
car dealership, and Sherry's mother's job was caring for Sherry
and her two little sisters.

Throughout the elementary grades, Sherry loved school.
When she entered junior high, she continued to earn good
grades, had many friends, and was an ardent softball player.
Sherry, now almost 18, shared her story:

*I never took drugs or smoked, never anything like that
until I met the father of my baby. Then I became real
rebellious. We dated for a year, and my parents decided
we were getting too serious so they said I couldn't see him
any more.*

At that point I turned into a terrible person. I would lie, I'd not come home, I'd sneak out, and I fought with my parents constantly.

Two months later I told them I was pregnant..

They weren't mad, just very very disappointed. They were also surprised because they had absolutely no idea I was sexually active. This had never crossed their minds. They were shocked, and they and my little sister went to counseling a month or two later trying to deal with the whole thing.

But they never yelled. That wouldn't have helped anyway. They gave me options. At first they said I could either move out with the baby, or I could stay home and place the baby for adoption. They didn't think it would be right to have the baby at our house.

I didn't want adoption, and if I had moved out, I would have had to go on welfare. So I didn't make a decision.

Three weeks later they said they wanted an answer. We talked a long time, and finally they added the option of marriage.

I got pregnant in June and married Lou three months later. The following week I enrolled at New Futures. I transferred here because I didn't want to face my peers. I was afraid of what people would say. The day care and the small classes at New Futures appealed to me. Once I got here, I realized the most important part is the sup-port—if you have a problem, somebody will help you. We have lots of opportunities here to iron over the mistakes we've made. They push us, and they're ready to watch us make something of ourselves.

That first year was pretty good. Lou and I got along, and Danny was born on Valentine's Day. Then in June, after Lou graduated, we moved to another city, and that's when things got rocky.

I always had somebody to take care of me,
and now I'm alone.

Lou's mother died, he didn't like his job, and then, to
my complete shock, he started hitting me. He turned out to
be somebody I didn't want. He beat me up. He threw me
out. Once he abandoned me for three weeks with no
money and no car. Finally I said I had had enough. I
couldn't raise Danny in an environment like that.

Soon after all this started, we moved back to Albuquerque. Three months later we decided to get a divorce. Our
marriage wasn't working, so Danny and I moved into a
tiny apartment.

Danny will be two this summer. He's a neat kid, but he
takes a lot of time, tons of time. He loves the nursery here
at school, and he loves the teachers. He talks about them
all the way home and all the way back to school.

It's still very hard. I take Danny to see his dad, and
when we leave, he cries. I cry, too, all the way home. I
always had somebody to take care of me, and now I'm
alone.

Sometimes I feel like lying in bed and soaking in my
distress. But I know if I lie there I'll be even more miser-
able. When I come to school and am around people who
like me and think I can do something, I feel better. So I get
up and go.

It took me a long time to get the strength to do that.
Right after we decided to divorce, I stayed home for two
weeks, and I cried and cried.

I'm back at New Futures, and I'll graduate this
spring—much to my parents' surprise. They never thought
I'd make it. I wouldn't have without the day care here at
New Futures. I like my job, but I'm going on to community
college to study computers next fall.

Why Do Teens Get Pregnant?

Each teen parent is different from the others. Some have
"nice" families; others have been moved from foster home
to foster home throughout their lives. Young fathers include
the football star and the unemployed dropout. Parenthood
too soon is likely to be difficult for all of them.

Why do teens become pregnant? Caroline Gaston, principal of **New Futures School, Albuquerque, New Mexico,** described some of the reasons in *Our Troubled Teens* (1987: Generation at Risk), pages 28-30:

- **Lack of self-esteem and self-confidence.** Self-esteem and self-confidence play important roles in teen sexual behavior. A teen with low self-confidence finds it difficult to say "No" to pressure from a boyfriend or girlfriend. Teens with low self-esteem may enter into sexual activity because it makes them feel that someone loves them.
- **Hopelessness about the future.** Many young people feel quite hopeless about their futures. Those who have no hope for a good life in the future believe it makes little difference how they behave. They believe in seeking pleasure for the moment.
- **Dysfunctional families.** Many families find themselves in such difficult economic and/or emotional circumstances that it is difficult for them to provide guidance or emotional support for their children.
- **Media influence.** The media—primarily radio and TV—bear a heavy responsibility. Listen to the words of the music on any radio station which targets the adolescent audience. Watch MTV, and listen to the words. Watch a few evenings of prime-time television and note the number of sexual innuendoes, references to unmarried sexual activity, unmarried pregnancies, and other indications that "everybody's doing it." The most powerful means of communication in our society are giving teens strong messages about sex.
- **Teens as risk-takers.** Teens are risk-takers. Psychologists who have studied the development of thought processes in young people report that teens seldom believe that anything bad will happen to them. Most teens think that pregnancy happens only to others. This psychological attitude affects teen behavior in a number of areas including adolescent pregnancy.
- **Teens may feel planning to be sexually active is wrong.** Many teens do not want to plan ahead to be sexually active

because they believe that early sexual activity is wrong. They believe, consciously or subconsciously, that if sex happens "naturally," without pre-planning, it's okay, or at least just a mistake, not a sin.

- **Inability to discuss birth control with sexual partner.** Often in this society, young women fear being labeled "sleazy" by their partner if they show knowledge of or have birth control.
- **Parents not comfortable talking about sex.** Many parents are not comfortable talking to their children about sex, so teens may not get the information and guidance they need from their families.
- **Teens fear that parents will find out.** Some teens fear that if they use birth control, their parents may find out about it and be very angry with them. If parents know they're sexually active, perhaps they won't be able to go out, or may not be allowed to see a boyfriend/girlfriend. Some even fear physical abuse from such anger. Fear of parents' anger is much more immediate, and therefore greater, than a teen's fear of getting pregnant in some dimly-defined future.

---

*The teen, male or female,
who wants to say "No" to sexual intercourse
may get little support.*

- **Different standards for young men.** The double standard still exists in today's society. Some people still believe, "It's okay for a young man to sow a few wild oats," placing all the responsibility to say "No," or to use birth control, upon the young woman.
- **Young teens' inability to plan ahead.** Teens, especially younger teens, are still in the developmental stage in which planning ahead is difficult. To think only in the here-and-now is their typical way of operating. Talking with teens in this stage about the consequences of their behavior often means very little to them.

- **Peer pressure.** Much of society, in addition to the media, seems to be saying to teens, "Everybody's doing it. There must be something wrong with you if you don't." The teen, male or female, who wants to say "No" to sexual intercourse may get little support. Peer pressure is often involved when a teen becomes sexually active.
- **Contraceptive methods sometimes not accessible.** Contraceptive methods may not be readily accessible to some teens. Clinics may be open only during school hours. Teens may not have transportation to the clinic. They may not have the money to pay for birth control. Inaccessibility can also be psychological as well as geographical or financial.
- **Idle time.** Youth are mobile, and often have an abundance of "hanging-out time," especially if they are not in school or are unemployed. Parents are often absent from the home. Studies indicate that conception takes place most often in the home of the young woman or man.

To be able to give birth may represent her only feeling of achievement.

- **Lack of information.** Some teens have too little information or inaccurate information about the human reproductive cycle and about effective methods of contraception or about where or how to obtain them.
- **Pressure on adolescents to be adult.** Many young men feel pressure to have sex—perhaps even to father a child—in order to prove their masculinity and to acquire adult status. If a young man cannot get a job, this may be one of the few ways he sees to prove his manhood. A young girl may equate being a mother with being a woman; to be able to give birth may represent her only feeling of achievement.
- **Parent-teen problems.** Many teens have stormy relationships with their parents. Having sex may be a

way to rebel against parents. Having a baby may be
seen as a way to become independent, or to overcome
objections to a boyfriend or girlfriend.

- **Drug and alcohol influence.** A significant amount of
  teenage sexual activity occurs when teens are under the
  influence of drugs or alcohol and inhibitions are
  relaxed.
- **Unhappiness.** Some teens feel so much despair,
  bewilderment, or frustration about their present situations that almost anything looks better to them. They
  may believe that having a baby may bring them closer
  to their parents, enable them to create a happy family,
  or to experience love.
- **Desire to have someone love them.** Some teens want,
  consciously or subconsciously, a child so that there
  will be another human being close to them who loves
  them.
- **Lack of knowledge about parenting responsibility.**
  Few teens understand the real, twenty-four hours a day
  responsibility of being a parent. Without this knowledge, it is difficult for them to make a decision about
  becoming a parent.

"My Life Was Falling Apart"

Alyce is a lovely dark-haired Native American who grew up
in Idaho. Her story is unique—just as every teen parent's story
represents a unique life.

She explained why she moved from her home to another
state, and talked about the changes in her life since her
daughter's birth:

> *My life was falling apart. I was doing drugs. I was with
> all these guys, and I got a disease. I got kicked out of
> school when I was in eighth grade. I was in a fight with
> two girls against me, and in the fight I hit the teacher. So I
> was kicked out.*
>
> *I decided I can't do this, I have to get away from these
> people around me. The only way I could do that was to*

*come down here with my aunt. And there's been a
dramatic change in me.*

*I got pregnant at a powwow in Washington when I was
still taking drugs. My aunt and her husband travel all over
the country and entertain at powwows. I'm Shoshoni, and
I love to meet people. Every weekend it was a powwow in
a different place.*

*My baby's dad was always doing drugs. That's what we
had in common. But I haven't seen him since the day I got
pregnant. I was fifteen then.*

*The night I realized I was pregnant I was smoking
marijuana. Then I decided I wanted a healthy baby, so I
quit. I was wishing for something to change my life
around, and Heather did it.*

I want my baby to have nice things.
You see, I don't have anything right now.

---

*When I realized I was pregnant, I transferred to the
teen parent program. I don't know what I'd have done
without it—I wouldn't have known anything about my
pregnancy or how to take care of Heather.*

*All during my pregnancy my aunt and uncle would
bring me down here to the pueblos for the dances. We'd
also have these ceremonies every weekend, like church,
and it's called sweats.*

*That's where I met my boyfriend Marshall. I was five
months pregnant.*

*That's also how I got to be friends with Curtis and
Lucia, where I live now. I'd spend weekends with them
when I was pregnant. I could get a lot of rest there
because they don't have any children.*

*My aunt gave me a chance. We have had some prob-
lems, too, though, so the day after Heather was born, I
moved in with Curtis and Lucia. My mom wanted me to
finish high school, and Curtis said they would take me in
and help me graduate, with the condition that they have
guardianship over me.*

*My boyfriend Marshall loves my baby so much. I tried
to break up with him once, and he said he'd take Heather.*

*I bring her to school every day. I feed her and change
her diapers. Once in awhile when I have homework, Lucia
will help me. And once in a great while I get impatient
when Heather won't go to sleep, and Lucia will rock her.*

*Heather's father knows about her. Word travels. We
call it the powwow trail. My grandma lives in Oregon, and
they were at a powwow up there somewhere. She saw
James' father and she ran up to him and threw her arms
around him and called him Grandpa. James tried to come
see me but he had car trouble. I'm glad they made an
effort to come. If Heather wants to know her father, I
don't mind. My boyfriend Marshall is still Daddy. James
is her father.*

*I want to go on to school and get a good paying job. I
want my baby to have nice things. You see, I don't have
anything right now. The most valuable thing I have is my
outfit, my beaded outfit. I want my baby to have a good
life.*

*Marshall wants to get married right out of high school,
but I told him no. I probably sound selfish, but I told him if
he really loves me, he can wait.*

*It's hard, this Indian way. You're trying to be tradi-
tional but you have to live in this world. My uncle told me
there is a red road and a white road. The red road is the
right way and the white road is the wrong way. Every day
you pray you can stay on that red road. Right now I think
I'm pretty much on that red road, but last year I was on
the white road and I had a lot of problems.*

"I Don't Want Him Calling Someone Else Dad"

Kenny, nineteen, whose son Travis is two, participates in the
Maine Young Father's Project. His story, too, is unique, but
provides insight into the problems many teenage fathers must
confront.

Kenny quit school in eighth grade, and has had a couple of
stints in the Job Corps. His father died before he was born, and

his mother, who had ten children, was always a single parent. Kenny recalled:

> *I was into drugs a lot, and still am. I grew up with a lot of problems. My stepfather beat me and I don't want my son to have that. Travis has brought happiness into my life. I see him twice a week, as much as I can, because I don't want him calling somebody else Daddy. That would hurt me a lot.*
>
> *Even if his mother gets married, I don't want Travis calling some other man Daddy, so I'm going to try to stick around. I have to pay the state—it costs me $400 a month to support him.*

Kenny commented on the Young Fathers Group:

> *It's helped me with some of my problems. We learn what rights we have—I didn't know I had any rights at all with my son. I didn't know if I left my girlfriend I would have any chance in the world to have custody of my child. The way I grew up, the mother always had custody, and I didn't know any different.*
>
> *In the group we can let our feelings out, talk about what's going on in our lives. Another guy is going through the same things I am. I can ask him how he's doing, and he asks me how I'm doing.*
>
> *Travis' mother has it in her mind that all men are evil. Her father beat her and he shot her mother. When she was ten years old, she had a boyfriend who was thirty-five, and she was living on the streets when she was fourteen. It's going to take a lot for her to get over these problems. She doesn't trust me, and I've never done anything to make her not trust me.*
>
> *I resent my mother. She always had time for other people but never for me. I never had any support at all. It was always "Get the hell out of the house so I don't have to deal with you."*
>
> *Every one of my brothers has been arrested at least once, and one is in prison now for murder. I've never been*

arrested in my life, but I have never gotten any praise for that. We very rarely celebrated a birthday.

Travis' mother reminds me more and more of my mother, and I think maybe that's why I resent her so much.

Represent All Segments of Society

Teen pregnancy touches all segments of our society. All geographic areas, rural and urban, all socio-economic strata, and all ethnic and religious groups are impacted. No group is immune.

The majority of young people caught in early parenting, like Sherry, Alyce, and Kenny, love their children and want to be good parents. Many, like Sherry, undoubtedly feel like "lying in bed and soaking in my distress."

As you consider what you can do to reduce teen pregnancy, think of Sherry—or the girl next door or the boy down the street—instead of thinking of those million teenagers getting pregnant or the 470,000 delivering babies. Look at the lives of young people in your community, beyond the charts and numbers. They are your teen pregnancy challenge.

The best way to help those young people on your street, across town and throughout the country is to provide services designed to *prevent* too-early pregnancy, and to deliver those services early and on a continuing basis. Parents have a lot to do with that part of it. So do the churches, the schools, the health and social service agencies, and the entire community.

There is something everyone—every individual and every organization—can do to reduce unintended teen pregnancy. To decide what you can and need to do in your community, start first with your vision.

CHAPTER 2

Starting
With the Vision

Our country was founded by people of great vision and inspiring dreams. They looked to a future bright with promise and hope. Each generation brought new ideas and creative approaches to meet current needs and move toward future goals. Challenges stimulated their thinking and fueled their ability to bring about change.

Today in our high-tech, computerized society, we struggle with a staggering array of pressing human needs. Somehow we seem to have lost our sense of direction—our vision. Many social problems simply appear too overwhelming, too complex, too costly, or too controversial to address effectively, if at all.

The programs offered in response to these problems are often described as band-aid efforts that are too little and too late to have any lasting impact.

Adolescent pregnancy continues to be identified as a significant problem with staggering costs and consequences at the local community, state and national levels. The related social

problems are multiple, and include school failure, poverty, unemployment, medical complications, welfare dependency, and
children at risk from poor parenting.

Increased public awareness in recent years has placed
adolescent pregnancy on many organizational and community
agendas. Moving beyond agenda item status to action may prove
difficult as we grapple to get to the root of the problem. We must
then identify and build support for appropriate program
responses.

Adolescent pregnancy issues are viewed by many people as
controversial, costly, divisive, or impossible to resolve. Instead
of looking for the common ground issues as a starting point,
areas of disagreement may surface immediately. These can pile
one upon another at the starting point, leaving the common
ground issues as the ultimate but distant goal.

Defining Our Vision

Widely divergent groups can find some areas of agreement.
Both pro-life and pro-choice groups prefer that young people not
get pregnant before they are able to support and care for a child.
We all want children and teenagers to grow into self-sufficient
adults. We want young people to develop high self-esteem and a
strong sense of belonging. We want to help increase young
people's chances of having successful and happy lives.

What is your vision of the ideal environment for young
people and their families in your community? Starting with a
vision of the ideal situation enables you to identify and
emphasize the common ground ideas of self-respect, caring,
self-sufficiency, and hope.

Your vision may also include:
- **Children** who are valued, nurtured, wanted and loved.
- **Teenagers** who have been helped to develop a strong
  sense of self-worth and belonging, who have been provided information and support in making positive life decisions, and who have a sense of responsibility for their
  actions.
- **Parents** who are prepared to be the primary family life
  educators for their children, who place parenting as a high

priority in their lives, who continually seek to develop their parenting and communication skills.

- **Families** which are loving, caring, stable units where all family members are valued, have a role, and a sense of importance and belonging.
- **An educational system** which is nurturing and enabling, one which provides a process for developing self-esteem and a sense of self-worth so young people believe they have an important role in society.
- **Religious groups** which are involved in sexuality education for young people and families.
- **A business community** which values parenting, recognizes the strength of secure family life, and supports family needs in the workplace.
- **A health care system** which promotes prevention and wellness and is available to everyone.
- **Media** which promote positive family values and responsible role models.
- **Government** which exhibits a genuine concern for people and their well-being and a responsiveness to the needs of young people and their families.

Your vision defines the ultimate goal and mission of your program.

The real challenge begins when this vision is translated into an action plan for the present. The action plan maps out the specific program outline, what the program will do and whom it will serve, as well as how the program will be structured, implemented, and funded.

Prevention to Care Continuum

Ideally, each community would provide a coordinated, comprehensive continuum of services. These services would be designed first to prevent too-early pregnancy, and second, to help alleviate the problems faced by teens already pregnant or parenting.

It may be helpful to think of adolescent pregnancy in terms of a *continuum of prevention,* with numerous points along the continuum for possible intervention.

Continuum of Prevention

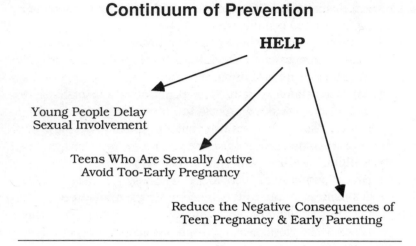

HELP

Young People Delay
Sexual Involvement

Teens Who Are Sexually Active
Avoid Too-Early Pregnancy

Reduce the Negative Consequences of
Teen Pregnancy & Early Parenting

A wide variety of tested intervention programs and services
can be considered for each point on the continuum of
prevention.

Start with the Parents

To keep teens from becoming sexually active, we can help
parents improve their skills in discussing sexuality issues and
communicating their values to their children. We need to make
family counseling readily available to help family systems work.

All of us—parents, teachers, anyone interacting with
children—must do all we can to help children improve their self-
confidence and self-esteem. We can provide a variety of opportunities for growth for all children, academically, physically,
and socially. Above all, we *must* give them a chance to succeed
at an early age and to reinforce continually that feeling of
personal success as they move toward adulthood.

An important part of children's growth is their attitude toward
their bodies and their sexuality. Parents, as the primary educators of their children, may need help in this area. **Family
TALKS** (Talking and Listening to Kids about Sexuality) is a
program developed by **Terry Reilly Health Services, Inc.**, of
Nampa, Idaho, to support parents of young children in their
role as the primary sex educators of their children. The three

two-hour sessions are designed for small groups of parents, and are conducted by trained leaders.

The program's content helps parents become more aware of children's feelings about themselves, and it helps parents promote positive self-images in their children. Through guided discussion, it provides skills with which parents can communicate their sexual values to their children, cope with the embarrassment which often arises from children's curiosity about sexuality, and reassure their children about their normal growth and development.

Ellen Peach, who co-authored the program with David Reese, commented:

> *Sexuality education is a lifelong process—children are thinking about differences in their bodies and where babies come from at a very early age. We started Family TALKS because back in 1978 everybody was saying sexuality education was somebody else's responsibility. The schools said it was the church's, the church said it was the family's responsibility. Then someone said, "Wouldn't it be nice if parents learned to talk to kids earlier than during the teenage years?"*
>
> *So we started with a church group. Next we went to a day care group, then to the community ministerial council, and then it was a PTA, all parents of little kids. The parents gave us tremendous feedback on what they liked and what they needed. We realized that, because society doesn't see little children as sexual, parents are willing to talk with them. They're willing to be open. It was a real grassroots program with tremendous input from the parents.*
>
> *From working with the parents directly, we went to training parents, then to the training of trainers. This meant the program would keep going.*
>
> *There's a version for Native Americans. They put some of the Navajo sayings and designs all through it. We also worked with the Yu'Pik Eskimo in Bethel, Alaska. Since we're not of that culture, we said, "Look, this is yours.*

You take it and do as you feel necessary to meet the needs of parents."
    This program is a catalyst, a gentle way to get communities to look at these issues.

Vicki Tollefson, Salem, Oregon, and her husband participated in Family TALKS when their sons were two, four, eight, and ten years old. Now she is a leader of parent groups. She recalled:

I never ever would have talked to my parents about sexuality issues. I guess the advantage of having been involved in Family TALKS is keeping the bridge of communication open, being able to talk with the kids about all kinds of topics. Parents who can talk with their kids about sex are more likely to think it's okay to talk about other things.
    The class is geared to people with little children. We ask the parents, "How did you learn about sex? Do you want your children to learn in the same way?" Usually they want something different for their kids.

This is one example of ways to help parents become the primary sex educators of their children. Other programs have been organized by churches, PTAs, schools, and health and social agencies. None, unfortunately, reach all parents of young children.

Delaying Sexual Involvement

We can focus on helping all young people—from an early age on—to succeed and to develop a strong sense of self-worth. In a variety of ways we can support teens who say "No" to sexual involvement. We can teach teens the skills to handle peer pressure and to say "No" to potentially risky behavior. We can help them learn decision-making skills to use as they make critical life choices.

Dropping out of school is tied closely to low self-esteem. We can analyze practices and attitudes within our schools which may lead children and teens to have low self-esteem. When we identify these practices and attitudes, we must find ways to change them. In doing so, we may be able to reduce the school dropout rate.

In her mind, if she has a baby,
she will have something
and feel she is somebody.

Falling behind a grade or more in school is a predictor of school failure which in turn may lead to teen pregnancy and other at-risk behaviors. We need to double our efforts at early identification of the young people who aren't doing well in school. We must provide creative programs to keep them enrolled and help them achieve success.

Parents of elementary school students need access to parenting education. If parents are to be supported as the primary educators of their children, providing the help many of them want and need is essential.

We can provide education about parenting responsibilities to teenagers, including peer presentations from teen parents about the realities of their life situations. In addition, teens need accurate information about how reproduction occurs and how to prevent it.

We also need to provide youth with appropriate training for meaningful work and self-sufficiency. A good way to help these young people learn and use decision-making skills so important in the prevention of too-early pregnancy is to help them develop adequate skills for gainful employment and a satisfying life. The young man who knows he has a future may be willing to help delay his partner's pregnancy until he is able to follow the Urban League poster advice: "Don't make a baby if you can't be a father."

These are a few ways we can work toward providing hope and positive life options for all young people. This is the foundation upon which all our efforts at preventing teenage pregnancy must rest. These needs must be reflected in the mission statements of local school districts and other youth-serving groups.

A young woman who feels she has nothing may see no
reason to delay pregnancy. In her mind, at least if she has a
baby, she will have *something* and will feel she is *somebody*.
Our job is to help her—and her partner—find alternatives to
too-early pregnancy.

Emphasizing Primary Prevention

The **Postponing Sexual Involvement (PSI)** series from the
Teen Services Program, Grady Memorial Hospital, Atlanta,
Georgia, was designed for youth thirteen to fifteen years of age.
PSI is designed to help them identify and develop assertive skills
to resist social and peer pressure to become sexually active
before they're ready. PSI is a primary prevention program which
has been incorporated into hundreds of local community settings
across the country from school systems to housing projects.

The curriculum was co-authored by Marie E. Mitchell, Coordinator of the Teen Services Program, and Marion Howard,
Associate Professor at Emory University School of Medicine
and Director of the Teen Services Program, Grady Memorial
Hospital, Atlanta, Georgia.

PSI also provides "Postponing Sexual Involvement, An
Educational Series for the Parents of Young Teens," a three-
hour program designed for parents of students enrolled in PSI.
The session is designed to help parents:

- Understand the pressures in our society which influence
  young people's sexual behavior.
- Learn skills they can share with their young teens to aid
  them in postponing early sexual involvement.

In the Atlanta public schools, PSI is part of a series of ten
classroom sessions designed to provide eighth grade youth, male
and female, with basic factual information about human sexuality and decision-making, and to improve the skills of youth in
dealing with peer pressure that may lead them into early sexual
involvement. The human sexuality component of the program
takes five classroom periods and is implemented by nurses and
counselors. The skill-building component—when participants
discuss the pressures to have sex and learn assertive techniques
for postponing sexual involvement—takes five sessions and is

taught by eleventh and twelfth grade teen leaders under
supervision of the PSI coordinator.

Joseph Richburg, a teen leader in Atlanta, explained, "The
kids tell us they appreciate us coming. We're there for five
sessions, and trust develops during that time. We use three
assertive techniques for saying 'No.' The first is to keep saying
'No' with no excuses. The second is to tell the person who is
pressuring you how the pressure makes you feel. The third
technique is to walk away from the pressure.

"Sometimes fathers actually encourage their sons to be
sexually active," Richburg mused. "We tell teenagers there are
lots of other ways to prove their manhood."

Another peer leader, a young woman, explained, "I got
involved because a lot of my friends and people younger than
me were getting pregnant. I said, 'Something has to be done. We
can't have all these girls getting pregnant.' So I felt it would be
important to let teenagers know it's not only the adults telling
you to postpone sexual involvement—some teenagers do too.
Perhaps they could relate better to someone their own age"

Mitchell, coordinator of the program, commented:

*Our program philosophy is that most teens under
sixteen, because of their physical, emotional, and cogni-
tive development, have not developed the skills necessary
to make decisions about their sexual behavior. For that
age group, the best option is to postpone sexual involvement. By the time they're sixteen, they're more likely to be
able to look at the consequences, to be able to handle the
decision-making and the responsibility.*

*What I like most about the series is that young people
respond so positively to it. Sometimes we think kids just
naturally have sexual intercourse. We as adults seem to
say, "Gee, this is something kids are going to do." But I
think kids are interested in having the abstinence option
discussed.*

*They seem to want adults to say these things to them,
particularly those kids who don't want to be sexually
involved. Sometimes we're so concerned with prevention*

that we simply put a birth control clinic in an accessible
place and expect that to take care of things.

We clearly say PSI is not a complete sex education
program. It's designed to do only one thing, to teach kids
to resist the pressure toward early sexual involvement.

Some people use this as a way to get around the other
issue of birth control. It's hard to get society to think
about kids needing a variety of options—that "No" is an
option for some kids, but for others, it's not. Those other
kids need the option of birth control. For those for whom
birth control doesn't work, other supportive services
are needed.

Research shows a dramatic drop in sexual involvement of
eighth grade girls after taking the PSI course, according to
Mitchell. On the average, fifteen percent of eighth grade low-
income girls who receive no special program help become
sexually involved by the end of the school year. The Grady
Hospital program reduced this to five percent, a reduction of
about sixty-seven percent. In human terms, two out of every
three girls who ordinarily might have become sexually involved
were assisted in postponing such involvement.

Kristin Ann Hardy, a PSI teen leader in Atlanta, wrote,
"When I present the PSI series, I feel as though I'm providing
those eighth graders with a weapon in this war against teenage
pregnancy. This weapon is the confidence to say 'No' to anything they do not want to do, especially having sex before
they're ready."

After-School Groups

Teen Talk, Winston-Salem, North Carolina, is a teen preg-
nancy prevention program of the Forsyth County Health
Department. It focuses on self-esteem, career exploration, and
pregnancy prevention. Currently directed by Patricia Minter,
Teen Talk was founded by Beth Harris Brandes, who now
coordinates a teen pregnancy prevention program through the
Catawba County Department of Social Services, Newton, North
Carolina.

Teen Talk is an after-school and summer program targeted for teenage women living in an area with an extremely high rate of adolescent pregnancy. The program, which meets every other week, was started in 1986 with eight girls and eight volunteers. By the end of the summer, eighty young women were participating. A similar program for males, Man Talk, started a few weeks later. Brandes discussed Teen Talk and the young women involved:

> *Most of the kids I work with have a very narrow vision of where they can go. They have a sense of hopelessness.*
>
> *Initially they came to Teen Talk out of curiosity. They had fun and they found adults who really listened to them. Over time, once they got hooked into the program, we began to introduce incentives to change their behavior. Certainly preventing pregnancy is one of the most complex things to effect. But we pointed out that you really are making a choice.*
>
> *The themes didn't change, but developmentally this age group needs to hear messages over and over before they can internalize them. We package the message in lots of different ways and repeat it.*
>
> *We use lots of experiential activity, making learning fun, playing "The Price is Right" with baby supplies, for example, or "Wheel of Fortune" with parts of the body. They love it.*
>
> *When Teen Talk started, they said the worst thing was to be a virgin. Over time there was a real shift, and two years later they felt sad when someone got pregnant.*

Avoiding Too-Early Pregnancy

Whatever we might prefer, some teens choose to be sexually active. Today, more than ever, they are responding to the heavy sexual messages that permeate much of our society—in TV, music, movies, videos, advertising, magazines, and other media.

Unfortunately, programs aimed at helping teens refrain from becoming sexually active are not enough. Whether we like it or not, many teens are sexually active. It is estimated that one in five girls and one in three boys is sexually active by age fifteen, with the average age of first sexual involvement at sixteen. Once started, many young people will continue to be sexually active. "Just say 'No'" is not likely to be a helpful approach for them.

For those teens already sexually active, a clear understanding of the responsibilities they must take for their actions is imperative. Limiting the implied choices to sexual abstinence or pregnancy is likely to result in more pregnancy. Instead, we need to help parents communicate with their teens about responsible sexual behavior, and young people need to be motivated to prevent conception until they are ready to parent a child.

Young people who are sexually active, both males and females, must have information about relationships, contraception, and avoiding unintended pregnancies. They must have access to counseling as well as contraception. They need health professionals, teachers, and other adults to give them accurate information, support them in making responsible decisions, and help them understand the consequences of their life choices.

Comprehensive Teen Health Centers

In Michigan sixteen comprehensive health centers for teens have been set up, with about half being located at schools, according to Karen Schrock, Chief of the Eastern Regional Division of the **Michigan Department of Public Health.** She explained:

>   We deliberately chose *"Comprehensive Teen Health Center"* as opposed to Teen Pregnancy Prevention Project because health needs of teens are so comprehensive. Each center develops its own policy through its community advisory board. They decide who can attend, and in some cases the dropout population is welcome.
>   Michigan law does not allow contraceptives to be distributed within schools, but clinic staff can do exams. Some clinics, housed outside the school building, write prescriptions. All clinics counsel and educate. If they can't do the prescriptions, they'll do the exam, then tell the teen, "Go to the Health Department to get your prescription."

*We have a prevention orientation. Our goal is to get
young people to delay the initiation of sexual intercourse.
Quite a few of our programs are trying to get young
people to say "No" to sex, but we know that won't be the
total solution. We're working on all fronts. Every survey
I've seen says that by the time an adolescent goes to a
family planning clinic, s/he is already sexually active.
Certainly if we can't prevent the first pregnancy, we're
working intensively to prevent the second one.*

The best of the adolescent health clinics know well that
information on human sexuality, contraception, and life planning cannot be delivered in a vacuum. In order to help young
people become whole human beings—physical, psychological,
and moral entities—they must be approached holistically.

Clinics or school settings which employ interdisciplinary
teams to interact with their young clients as well as among
themselves have the potential of helping young people develop
life planning skills in a comprehensive sense. Decisions about
sexual activity, contraception, or parenting then are placed in
perspective within the total framework of the young person's
individual world of reality.

Needs of Pregnant and Parenting Teens

Our vision of the ideal world probably does not include
pregnant and parenting adolescents. We know too much about
the adverse effects of too-early pregnancy. Reality, however,
necessitates the need for services to help reduce the negative
consequences for these young parents. For example, we need to
provide early and regular prenatal care which is accessible, low-
cost, and in a comfortable, caring environment for teens. Our
goal is to provide health education which gets young parents-to-
be involved in being good to their babies before they're born.
Adolescents provide a disproportionate share of the United
States' embarrassing record of infant mortality.

Pregnant teens and their partners need to be supported in
considering their pregnancy alternatives. They need the assistance and encouragement of caring adults to make the decisions

Hart Junior High, Washington, DC

appropriate for their life situations and to access available community resources. The community must make the completion of a high school diploma or its equivalency a goal for all students.

Young people need special services to help them stay in school throughout pregnancy and afterward—and to help them come back to school if they've already dropped out. School personnel must be sensitized to the needs of pregnant and parenting students.

In a school system, attitudes of top school administrators set the tone. Sensitivity and understanding among school administrators varies dramatically even within the same general area. An administrator in a large school district in northern Virginia (considered to be very progressive) remarked, "The taxpayers don't want to pay for homebound instruction for teen parents. After all, they *chose* to get pregnant." You can almost hear the patronizing, judgmental tone, and, as we might expect, no program for pregnant teens exists in this district.

Contrast this comment with that of Kenneth Milner, Principal at **Hart Junior High** in nearby **Washington, DC,** whose school provides child care for student parents. Milner called the child care center "extremely important," then added:

> *We shouldn't condemn these young people and just*
> *leave them somewhere. We should educate them so it*
> *won't happen again. Most of the girls understand they've*
> *made a mistake, and they know they have to live with it.*
> *We're doing everything we can to help them become*
> *viable citizens, to give them a second chance.*

The Center's director, Millian Harrison, says the principal's support has been crucial to the success of the center. "He shapes the attitude for the school, and he's created a climate where the teachers and staff are very supportive of our program," she said.

Importance of Child Care

Accessible and low/no cost child care is imperative for many teen parents to complete their education. Their alternative is to leave school, perhaps forever. An important benefit in child care programs for teen parents is the opportunity for teens to learn how to parent well. Parenting education is essential for the ninety-six percent of teen mothers who keep their children, and for the fathers of those children. Unfortunately, many adolescents do not have good models of parenting, as they come from conflicted, stressful, or abusive home situations. Good parenting skills are not instinctive to many parents, but good parenting can be learned.

Teens enrolled in the **Young Families Program (YFP), Billings, Montana,** spend half their day at a special center and half in a regular school. The school-age parents can bring their children to the Parenting Center, a renovated house donated by Deaconess Medical Center, by 7:30 a.m.

The teen parents participate in parenting classes, group and individual counseling, self-esteem activities, health care instruction, and supervised time with their children. They are transported to the regular junior and senior high schools for their academic classes.

YFP teacher Marge Eliason feels this program model offers several important advantages:

* Keeps pregnant teenagers and teenage parents, male and female, in the educational and social mainstream.
* More educational opportunities and less isolation for the teen parents than an alternative school can provide.
* High-quality child care for students' infants with students having hands-on time with children.
* Parenting instruction in a natural setting.

Many Needs of Teen Parents

Vocational education and employment training are important for all young people, and absolutely essential for those undertaking the immediate responsibilities of parenting, both males and females.

Because the needs of teen parents are manifold, resourceful administrators have many avenues to pursue for support. The **Margaret Hudson Program for Schoolage Parents, Tulsa, Oklahoma,** has preserved an emphasis on vocational training and career counseling by combining the resources of vocational education through the public schools and federal assistance through the Private Industry Training Council administered by city government.

The funds from the city provide two counselors for students who qualify below the poverty level. They hold a group class once a week, and counsel students individually, with an emphasis on dropout prevention and remedial education, as well as establishing a career track. The vocational school funds pay salaries for the child care teacher, the vocational home economics teacher, and the business teacher, as well as one related academic teacher. Three teacher aides also come from this source. Social workers in the Margaret Hudson Program also help young parents in seeking employment.

In addition, there are many related issues important to the development of successful family units such as housing, transportation, health care for parents and their children, support groups for teen parents, and assistance in accessing community resources.

Teen parents also need help in avoiding further untimely pregnancy. They need counseling to assist them in dealing with the problems which may have led to the pregnancy or which may impede their ability to parent their children adequately. They are thrust rapidly from adolescence into adult responsibilities, and they need help to effect this transition.

Look for the Possible

The way we look at teen pregnancy may be somewhat like the analogy of looking at a half-filled glass of water. Is it half empty or half full? The teen pregnancy challenge facing every community represents significant and severe problems that need to be addressed. This challenge also offers an endless array of possible program interventions.

Whether it's a Big Brother/Big Sister program providing a caring adult mentor and friend for a young person in need of a positive role model, or a service club operating a clothes closet filled with maternity and baby outfits, there are programs that can be effective in your community.

Certainly some communities are better positioned to meet the challenge. They have committed leadership, a healthier economic base, a strong school-parent-community partnership, and the necessary resources. In other places, the challenge is more difficult, especially in areas locked in desperate poverty, apathy, and depleted resources.

In either case, however, little happens until someone or some group defines their vision of the way things ought to be . . . and starts moving forward. If we want young people to have a hopeful, healthy future, we must first model that hope for their future. It starts by asking, "Why not?" instead of just "Why?"

It starts with your vision.

CHAPTER **3**

Documenting The Need

"Teen pregnancy isn't a problem here."
The person making this statement may truly believe teenagers aren't getting pregnant in his/her community. She may tell you, "They're all getting abortions, you know." He may have the stereotypical view that too-early pregnancy happens only in certain socio-economic and ethnic groups. He may feel it's only the girl's problem. Or, her attitudes may take a punitive view: "After all, she chose to get pregnant. Let her deal with it."

First, teen pregnancy probably occurs in every community population which includes teens.

Second, it's doubtful that "everybody" is getting an abortion. Abortion is more likely to be used in some socio-economic and ethnic groups than in others. However, even in affluent neighborhoods, babies are still being born to teenagers not yet ready to parent.

Third, the teenage mother may appear to be more directly impacted by the negative consequences of a too-early pregnancy, but the consequences for the teen father can also be serious.

Lastly, few teens really choose to be pregnant. They are the victims of a society that saturates their world with sexual messages, telling them to "go for it." Or the girls may be hearing, "Just say 'No,'" while the boys' message is, "Hey, prove you're a man. Do it."

Considering the Facts

In the United States, a teenager is four times more likely to become pregnant than are teenagers in Sweden and France, and twelve times more likely than teens living in Japan, according to the November, 1988, "Facts at a Glance" (Child Trends, Inc.). According to the Alan Guttmacher Institute, if current trends continue, four of every ten fourteen-year-old girls in this country today will be pregnant at least once before they reach twenty.

More than 470,000 babies were born to teenagers in 1986, thirty-eight percent (178,748) to women aged seventeen or younger. Sixty-one percent of these babies were born to unmarried women. Of babies born to mothers younger than fifteen, 13.8 percent weighed less than five and a half pounds, high-risk by definition.

Two-thirds of the children younger than three in the United States live in households headed by fifteen to twenty-one-year-olds who are poor. Of women who had their first child while in their teens, and who were unmarried at the time of delivery, three-fourths received welfare at some time during the four years after the birth, according to *Teenage Pregnancy: An Advocate's Guide to the Numbers* (1988: Children's Defense Fund).

The need for teen pregnancy prevention programs and for services for adolescent parents seems obvious when the human costs and the dollar costs are carefully examined.

"Not in My Community!"

Nevertheless, in some communities the problem is ignored. Some people still insist, "Not in my community!" For example, a school board member at a national conference in Anaheim,

California, was asked by a NOAPP member about services for pregnant students in his district.

"I guess you don't understand since you live out here in California," the school board member replied, "but we don't have pregnant girls in our school district. You see, I'm from Ohio, and we're in the Bible belt!"

This is a classic "head-in-the-sand" approach to teenage pregnancy . . . and it can be found in every region of the country.

Anyone wanting to develop a program either to prevent teenage pregnancy or provide services for teen parents in this man's district would need to do some careful data collecting to document the incidence of teenage pregnancy *in that community* and the related costs and consequences. Whether or not people in your community appear to be aware of the teen pregnancy challenge, documentation of need is required for any program proposal.

Beth Brandes, who developed the **Teen Talk** program in **Winston-Salem, North Carolina,** stressed the importance of documenting the need:

>*I feel strongly that first you do your homework and establish statistically where the greatest need is in your community. Then you go in and build your case with the people with whom you'll be working. In Forsyth County we looked for the highest rate of teen births by census tract and discovered the greatest need was within a mile of our Health Department. In addition to the data base, I've always tried to document where the gaps in services are—so people can't deny why this is going on here.*
>
>*Once you document the lack of services and make it clear you want to fill those gaps, you can generally get the backing of the professional community because they know you have no intention of encroaching on their territory.*

Accurately assessing local community needs is critical to the success of adolescent pregnancy care and prevention programs. Programs developed based on myths or stereotypes about adolescent pregnancy or the target population are destined for trouble from the beginning. Programs which duplicate existing efforts can waste valuable resources.

Barbara Huberman, Executive Director of the **North Carolina Coalition on Adolescent Pregnancy,** started their needs assessment with the community at-large rather than with service providers. She explained:

We wanted to know about existing services so we sent a nine-page questionnaire to two thousand people in the state. We got six hundred back and entered the results in the computer. From this we developed a list of what people said should be done and/or what they thought was lacking. Then, with the help of a consultant, we interviewed teenagers across the state.

Finally, we held a series of community meetings and did group presentations. Those attending these meetings were given the list of needs from that survey, and they ranked the services as to which were the most important. From that information we developed our service projects.

It Begins with You

Whether you're working as an individual, as part of a youth-serving agency, or as part of an existing coalition of organizations which addresses another youth-related issue, you can initiate a needs assessment in your community. The first step is to define the feelings or situations that created your awareness of a need.

A parent volunteer in an elementary classroom may feel that some of the children don't have a strong sense of self-esteem. A recreation director in a community center may feel the teen males need support as they begin making decisions about sexual activity.

A nurse in the maternity ward of the local hospital may notice that the number of younger teens giving birth has been increasing in recent years. A counselor in a city employment agency may find that many of the teen parents lack the basic skills they need to secure and hold jobs that provide enough money to support their families.

A teacher may be aware that a majority of the students who become pregnant drop out of school. A school board member may be concerned that the district is able to keep the students in school during pregnancy, only to have them drop out following delivery because there is no affordable infant care on or near the school campus.

Parents may find limited community services available to help their family when their sixteen-year-old daughter has an unplanned pregnancy. A pastor may have parents in the congregation indicate they want help in talking with their children about sexuality issues, perhaps an educational program within the church which addresses adolescent sexuality concerns.

The need you perceive may be a feeling, or it may be based on specific experiences. Either way, a good starting point is to write down what you see as the need and how you learned about the problem. Are you reacting to information from someone, or to personal experience? This will help you define the type of information you need to collect, and will give you clues about the specific target population. From there you need to determine where to go for information. Be aware, too, of other individuals and groups who might be interested in the problem, directly or indirectly.

Supporting Feelings with Facts

Once you have identified a need related to teenage pregnancy—wherever it is on the prevention continuum—the next step is to gather facts that present a clear picture of the problem from a total community perspective. When you start asking for information, you'll not only begin to compile data, but you will also begin to identify people who know what's going on, have access to resources, and may share your interest in the issue.

The need you have identified is probably only the tip of the iceberg. As you begin to look at the problem, you may find the issue is much larger and the potential for development of networks and resources much greater than you suspected—an exciting development.

"You have to start selling it to the community, not as a moral issue, but as a health and education issue," Marge Eliason,

Young Families Program, Billings, Montana, pointed out. "You have to do a needs survey because you'll have people saying, 'Oh, we don't have that many kids getting pregnant.'"

Eliason talked about the difficulties in doing such a survey. "So often teen parents vanish. So we started pulling kids in. They would come to meetings, and they'd tell us about other kids who had dropped out because of pregnancy. This was our core group. It was a core group without political clout, but they were the basis of our needs survey. Kids who had dropped out now said, 'I wish there'd been something for me.'"

"Once we got the numbers, we were ready to start building support for a program by establishing our advisory council," Eliason added.

Initiating a Needs Assessment

If there are no clearly identifiable programs, then your goal is to initiate a concrete assessment of the need for adolescent pregnancy prevention and care programs in the community. You need to know about programs currently available, where the gaps are, and what programs should be provided to fill the gaps. It's important to get the facts. Don't let myths and stereotypes become the basis for organizational decisions regarding adolescent pregnancy. The collection of well-documented factual information is absolutely critical when you're considering the development of a prevention or care program.

NOAPP's survey of successful prevention and care programs highlighted the need to gather accurate information about the problem at the beginning. When responding to the question, "Who collected the initial data?" answers ranged from "myself" to "volunteers and concerned citizens" to "a community committee." Who collects the data is not as important as which data are collected and where they are collected. Data collected may carry more weight if it's done as an activity involving an authorized committee or a collaboration of organizations.

First, be aware of the statistics concerning teenage pregnancy across the country and in your state. Good resources are "Facts at a Glance" by Kristin Moore and the Children Defense Fund's *An Advocate's Guide to the Numbers*. (Sources are listed in the

Appendix.) Most important, however, are the data from your community. Are these data already available? If someone has done the preliminary data gathering, you don't want to repeat this step.

There are a number of sources in every community for appropriate data—health departments, past and present program directors, teachers, counselors, hospital personnel, social service agencies, the local chapter of the March of Dimes, the United Way, the Census Bureau, and your state Department of Vital Statistics.

Incidentally, if you can't get the numbers you want in the way you want them, be persistent. For example, if the Department of Vital Statistics offers the number of babies born to mothers up to age nineteen, but you need births to women seventeen and younger, ask for those figures. They should be able to provide them.

Don't overlook interviewing the target audience—the teens themselves. The best planned program and best trained staff is of little value if the young people the program is designed to serve don't, can't, or won't use it.

Gathering the Data

The type of data collected should include the following:

- General demographic information for the community — total population, age and ethnicity of population, per capita income, economic base of the community, and population and economic trends over the past few years and for the coming decade.
- The number of pregnant teens and teen parents.
- The total number of births and abortions in the community each year, by age and race if possible.
- The number of teens in the community giving birth and the number having abortions over the past few years, broken down by age, ethnicity, socio-economic group, location.
- The number of repeat pregnancies to teen mothers.
- The number and percentage of premature, low birthweight births which occur for teens as compared to the number/percentage of high-risk births to non-teen mothers.

- Date of entry into prenatal care for pregnant teens.
- Infant mortality rates for babies born to teens.
- The percentage of infants in intensive care units of local hospitals whose mothers are teenagers.
- Health statistics for adolescents (i.e., sexually transmitted diseases, suicides, alcoholism, etc.) and related cost data.
- The dropout rate in the school district as a whole and by individual junior and senior high schools, with as detailed a profile as possible related to age, sex, ethnicity, and location.
- Information on existing adolescent pregnancy prevention or care programs.
- Interviews with pregnant or parenting teens (males and females) regarding their needs.
- Interviews with key community leaders representing education, health care, social service, religious, business, governmental, and volunteer sectors.

Finding School Dropout/Pregnancy Data

In our culture, education is a primary factor in determining life opportunities and success. You need to look carefully at the percentage and number of young people dropping out of school without earning a high school diploma. This number is probably far higher than the number the school gives as pregnancy-related dropouts.

In one survey of school administrators publicized across the United States, 74.2 percent said the dropout rate for pregnant and parenting students in their schools was three percent or less, another example of "head-in-the-sand" thinking. Research shows over and over again that at least half of all teen mothers in the United States fail to complete high school.

Failure to complete high school does not necessarily equal dropping out because of pregnancy. Some young women drop out before they get pregnant. The result is the same. They don't finish school.

Schools rarely have an accurate count of the numbers of young people who drop out because of pregnancy. Most estimates are low and misleading. Dropout may be attributed to poor school performance rather than the accompanying pregnancy. To get the number of births each year to teens, a good place to start is to check out the Vital Records Department of your local Department of Public Health. That's only *births*. You can probably double that number to estimate the number of pregnancies.

A teacher of a pregnant minor program was upset when she discovered several pregnant girls from the local high school had dropped out several weeks before they enrolled in the alternative program for pregnant students. "Why don't those counselors tell me when you leave because of pregnancy?" she asked her students.

"Oh, we don't tell them we're pregnant," several young women replied. "We tell them we're moving, or we simply quit going to school. They don't know where we are."

A nurse in an alternative school in southern California taught a prenatal health class in which eleven young women were enrolled. She knew that few pregnant or parenting students were enrolled in the district's other high schools.

The nurse was chagrined to learn from a newspaper story that 207 births to teenage mothers had occurred the previous year within her school district. She took the article to her principal and pointed out that they needed to expand their outreach program because so many pregnant teenagers in the district weren't coming to school.

"That's ridiculous!" the principal replied. "We know there are only eleven. That's how many you have, isn't it? Kids don't drop out of school because of pregnancy these days."

The principal, of course, was wrong. Many young women still leave school when they learn they're pregnant. They may not know it's illegal to push a student out of school because of pregnancy or marital status, so some assume they must leave. Others may not be able to participate in all the usual school activities, so decide to leave.

Some may be glad to have an excuse to quit school, not realizing the consequences of their actions. Or they may find that no one bothers to bring them back to school when their attendance starts falling.

On the other hand, teenagers who aren't pregnant may drop out of school due to lack of academic success or relevance to their lives. In fact, especially in communities with alternative schools, some decide to return to school *after* they become pregnant.

School programs for pregnant teenagers often find their enrollment includes a high percentage of young women back in school because they feel they finally have a reason to continue their education. School dropout statistics in your community will be an important part of your data collection.

Sherry Betts, Director of **Adolescent Family Education, Tucson, Arizona,** used these numbers to show her school district that the special program actually generated more money than its total expenses. (See *Teen Pregnancy Challenge, Book Two*, Chapter Nine.)

Go to your school district for statistics on the total number of students, males as well as females, who drop out of school. Ask for the number of students dropping out because of pregnancy. Then compare those figures with the total number of births to teenagers in the same area. You may unearth some extremely significant information.

Analyzing Existing Services

Look at *existing* services. Remember that many adolescent pregnancy prevention and care programs prefer to keep a low profile in the community and may not be readily apparent. (Keeping a low profile, however, generally means potential clients are not served because they don't know about the low-profile service.)

Sources of initial information about such programs include:
- United Way
- March of Dimes Birth Defects Foundation
- School administration including independent and home study programs
- Department of Public Health
- Ecumenical council
- Local or regional social service agencies
- Teen employment programs

- Area planning councils
- Local hospitals, especially the obstetrical and pediatric departments

If some adolescent pregnancy prevention or care services are currently provided, find out who is being served, the specific types of services being provided, their linkages with other groups and networks, the gaps in services they are not able to fill, and the groups or individuals who support their activities.

Are there ways to link with or support the existing programs to meet the identified need and begin filling the gaps in services? Is there an unnecessary duplication of services in some area? Time and time again, in small communities and in large, the lack of communication and community-wide planning results in major gaps in some areas, and a duplication of effort in others.

Chances are you'll find adolescent pregnancy in every socio-economic and ethnic group in your area. Too-early pregnancy is not limited to any particular kind of neighborhood or type of family, and stereotypes to the contrary need to be corrected.

Organizing the Data

You need to organize your data into a concise report which clearly outlines the problem to be addressed in your community. This report can be presented to key decision-makers to gain their support. It may be used to access groups who can develop resources.

It can also be used with local media to increase local awareness of the issue. Excerpts can be developed into local fact sheets and used in press releases.

Data will be most effective if both the human costs and the dollar costs to the community are outlined. For example, public awareness and support for care programs rose dramatically in one community when an adolescent pregnancy task force determined that half the infants in the intensive care unit of the county hospital were infants born to teen mothers. Translation: A large share of local tax dollars was being spent to pay for the medical needs of the infants of teen mothers. They knew this expense could be drastically reduced or prevented through

increased prevention efforts and better prenatal care for
pregnant teens.

The core group that collects the data needs to analyze the
dynamics of their community and determine the best strategy for
presenting the case to individuals and groups who have the
resources and contacts to make something happen. You continually need to bring other people into the information gathering
and program planning process.

If the primary leadership has been provided by service
professionals to this point, you need to begin involving some
key community figures and people who represent different
segments of the community. These community leaders can then
take the public role in presenting the case to decision-makers,
funders, and other audiences, and in mobilizing local resources.

Supporting the Need with Facts

A program's strength and viability over time depends in part
on the initial need the program was designed to serve. The need
must be real, it must be clearly identified, and it must be based
on facts.

There are many sources of reliable data in every community,
regardless of size. Remember always to start by looking at
existing data and services. Organize your data into a clear and
concise report or fact sheet that can be used throughout the
community to document the need for your proposed program.

The data gathering, analysis, interpretation, and dissemina-
tion becomes an on-going process as communities begin to
come to terms with adolescent parenting issues. The data base
becomes vital to measuring progress and outcome as programs
begin to expand to meet defined needs. In the computer age,
every community has the capacity for careful documentation.

Documenting the need can be a time-consuming process.
However, that process offers the opportunity to contact a lot of
people, introduce the issue, and begin building a base of community support. It's an important step in any program development process. Without the facts, it will be hard to convince
community leaders and potential funders that a problem exists.

Building Community Support

Once basic factual information has been collected, look again at your community. Is it traditionally supportive of youth-serving or charitable activities? Does the community look to outside forces to handle their problems, or is there a strong sense of "we can take care of our own problems?" What is the community attitude toward teen pregnancy—judgmental? ("Bad girls.") Or apathetic? ("We don't have a problem.")

Is there a strong volunteer network? Does the business community take an active role in addressing social issues? How involved is the religious community in initiating or supporting local programs targeting social service needs or the needs of young people? Do networks exist for communication and collaborative planning?

Adolescent pregnancy prevention and care programs meet with strong opposition in some communities. Prevention programs face conflicts over issues surrounding sex education, parental involvement, and values. Care programs must face

perceptions from some people that services for pregnant and
parenting teens encourage early sexual activity in the first place.
They may trigger judgmental attitudes such as, "Those girls
made a mistake and we shouldn't make things too easy for
them." Some may believe that such programs may be a public
embarrassment because they imply that someone failed
somewhere.

Successful programs work at combating negative perceptions
in an early and on-going manner. They build broad-based
community support and enlist recognized community leaders—
people with clout and contacts. They develop strategies to cope
with the sometimes active opposition of certain special interest
groups who may not even live in the local community. None of
this is easy.

Looking at Your Community

If your community does not have a visible track record of
local support and volunteer involvement in youth issues, you
will need to do some critical and creative analysis of the community structure. Questions to be asked in looking for sources of
potential community support are :

- What are the formal and informal power structures?
- Who are the people or groups that make things happen in
  the community?
- What groups have access to resources you might need?
- What are the major community priorities set by key governmental and civic groups? Do they include youth,
  families, education, health care, employment, or other
  issues which could be tied to adolescent programs?
- What existing agencies, organizations, or networks would
  be supportive of an adolescent pregnancy prevention or
  care program? What contacts does your initial group have
  with those organizations or networks?

Barbara Ziegler reported that the **Mecklenburg, North
Carolina, Council on Adolescent Pregnancy (MCAP)** began
by pinpointing community needs through a community awareness conference. Three hundred people representing businesses,
agencies, schools, communities, parents, clergy, medical people,

government representatives, and teenagers were invited to meet and discuss teen pregnancy.

Participants were given commitment cards to complete. "We asked for a commitment," Ziegler recalled. "They had several choices: 'Yes, I think this is a problem, but I don't have time to become involved' to 'Yes, this is a problem, and I'd like to be involved.'

"From these commitment cards we identified people who were willing to serve on various task forces, and these leaders became part of the twenty-five-member volunteer board of directors," she explained.

Building Linkages

Planning for effective coordination within the local community can be a difficult but essential task for successful program operation. No single program has all the resources for providing totally comprehensive prevention or care. In planning for the linkages with programs and services that will support your efforts, review the following:

- Is there a service climate supportive of community planning?
- Is there a history of successful planning and coordinating efforts?
- Is there a pattern of community coordination to address human service needs?
- Is there an existing experienced group of agency administrators and representatives who know each other well?
- Is there a stability in terms of organizations and workers?
- Is there physical proximity of the coordinating organizations?
- Is there a formal coordinating group such as the United Way or community planning system with established credibility?
- Do the agencies and organizations work together or are they sharply divided over turf areas?
- Do the schools, churches, businesses, volunteer groups, health/social service agencies, and the local government work together on human service or youth-related issues?

If these features exist, it will probably be easier for programs to gain the interagency support so necessary to provide the variety of services required for prevention of teenage pregnancy and for services for pregnant and parenting teens.

The local chapter of the **March of Dimes Birth Defects Foundation (MOD)** can be helpful in coalition building and coordination of services. Mary Hughes, National Vice President for Community Services for MOD, feels MOD can provide the link between the medical professional and the community organizations.

When asked the kind of help a program provider might expect from March of Dimes, Hughes replied:

> *You need to go to your local chapter and say, "You have a network in this community. I'd like you to provide me with that network because I need those services." That could be the most important thing we could offer. In addition, you should ask MOD for educational materials and for volunteer services. Offer to talk to their Health Professional Advisory Committee. Tell those volunteers about your services and how you're trying to upgrade them.*
>
> *You might say, "I have a service for pregnant teens in this community and I need help. How can you help me? What is your process for a grant? Do you have other resources? Do you have health professionals who might help me?"*
>
> *We need to talk creatively about the fact that we can't stick adolescents into a traditional health care system and expect it to work. We've got to reflect more intensely on how to make our present system more responsive to teen mothers.*

Presenting the Case

In gathering the factual information to document the need, you have identified individuals and groups interested in the issue. You are ready to begin using them. There is a role for everyone to play.

The core group which has collected the data and developed the initial program idea(s) now needs to determine the best strategies for presenting the case for these programs to individuals and groups who have the resources and contacts to make them happen and to bring other people into the program planning process.

This is often a difficult stage for the individuals who have been providing the initial leadership. In many instances, the primary leadership has come from service professionals who are familiar with the problem. At this point, however, it is critical for service providers to solicit the help of at least one key community figure who will take the lead public role in presenting the case and mobilizing community resources. The critical role for service providers then becomes that of enablers.

Some of the best community enablers are the ones who make sure others have ownership in the program and get the credit. It takes many people with many different talents and skills to develop and operate an effective adolescent pregnancy prevention or care program. As long as the initial vision is kept in the forefront and needs of young people are met, it shouldn't matter who winds up getting the credit.

Barbara Huberman, Chairperson of the **North Carolina Coalition on Adolescent Pregnancy,** stresses the need for a non-vested body:

> *This is critical. A service provider group may get the program started, but after awhile they may feel they have to protect their own program rather than continuing to look at it critically.*
>
> *Our emphasis here is to have a real community board so they can put the pressure on the school system or other community organization providing services to young people.*
>
> *Members of the community board are the policy makers, and they get things done. The school system cooperated when the chairman of the school board was on our board. If we had had only the teacher from the alternative school, this would never have happened.*

At the same time, involvement of service providers is also crucial. It is the teacher in the alternative school who may have the most realistic picture of the needs of young people. Her/his input is also important.

Working with Differences

To avoid dealing with a potentially controversial issue, political leaders may opt to avoid the issue altogether and pretend their community doesn't have a problem. They may feel the problem is not widespread enough to demand priority attention or resources. Worse yet, they may promote inaccurate stereotypes, indicating that it is only a problem among young people from a certain cultural, socio-economic, educational, or ethnic background.

Building community support on behalf of pregnant and parenting adolescents or for services dealing with prevention of adolescent pregnancy is difficult as well. Unlike other groups such as the handicapped, pregnant and parenting teens generally do not mount their own advocacy campaigns. Neither do their parents.

Often the groups advocating for services are service providers themselves, and sometimes policy-makers suspect such advocates of being self-serving.

Even successful programs with high visibility and strong community support continue to seek ways to deal with the sometimes fierce criticism directed toward them. Beginning programs must develop strategies to deal with such challenges or risk never getting started. They can learn from the experiences of others who have initiated similar programs in similar communities.

Adolescent Pregnancy Child Watch (APCW), Los Angeles, California, is a broad-based community coalition of service providers, school-based programs, public sector people, and others. One initiative of Adolescent Pregnancy Child Watch was the Los Angeles County Task Force on Teen Pregnancy. Included were representatives, for example, of Right to Life and Planned Parenthood. Jan Kern, APCW president, discussed the outcome:

> *The Board of Supervisors wanted everybody repre-*
> *sented, and it worked. Nobody wants teens to be pregnant,*
> *and as long as we stick to primary prevention, we can*
> *agree. There was very little problem. When you realize it's*
> *the future of our youth that's at stake . . .*
>
> *Building coalitions with diverse groups is a continual*
> *task and takes a long time. You have to build trust, and*
> *people have to be included from the very beginning. They*
> *can't be allowed to feel they're called on only when*
> *they're needed.*
>
> *Recently I was concerned about one individual, and I*
> *finally had lunch with her. I talked for ten minutes and she*
> *talked for fifty, and she's been with us ever since. Why*
> *didn't I think of that sooner? You can't take anyone for*
> *granted—that's the bottom line.*

Other programs surveyed indicated that they secured the
support of the mayor's wife, a key business leader, the bishop of
a major denomination, or an individual active in numerous local
fundraising endeavors to help present the data and their case to
key community leaders and the general public.

Countering Negative Attitudes

Sometimes community people express negative feelings
toward any kind of program dealing with sexuality or with
services for teen parents. It took Marge Eliason seven years to
get the **Young Families Program** started in **Billings, Montana.**
She talked about the negative reactions she at first encountered:

> *Yes, I ran into the same old lines. "If you give*
> *programs to these kids, we'll have more pregnancy."*
> *"You'll make it too easy for them and they'll stay on*
> *welfare all their lives." "They made their beds, let them*
> *lie in them."*
>
> *At one point, we thought we were set to go. Two*
> *school administrators told us the enrollment was way*
> *down at one of our junior highs. They were going to*
> *give us a room for the babies, a nice big old shop room*

which could have been fixed into a child care facility. It could have worked. We thought we were all set.

They even asked us if "those" girls would use the same bathroom.

Then we went to a parent advisory committee meeting. We walked in like babes in the woods. These people said, "You put those babies in that junior high and all those girls will come in and look at them, and they'll want to get pregnant." They even asked us if "those" girls would use the same bathroom. We were floored.

It was so unanticipated that we simply responded with the facts and figures. We told them we felt these babies needed to be nurtured and the mothers taught parenting skills, but they didn't hear us. All they heard was that "those girls" would be in their school.

We left hoping we could salvage the program.

About five weeks later our plan went to the school board, and suddenly there was no room, no money, nothing for our program. Of course the reason they gave us was money, but I'll never believe that. Those negative people got to the school board members.

So did we, but it wasn't enough. I made a call to every one of the board members, a personal visit, lunch. Some were on our wave length, but apparently others were not, and those sitting on the fence ran scared. So it didn't happen . . . and we realized the truth in the old maxim, "Politics may beat out all the rational planning you've done."

Three years later we got our program.

Today I don't hear those negative comments. Now I don't think it's popular to talk about "those girls" in Billings. It took a lot of time, a lot of patience, and a lot of hard work to get past that point.

In some cases, opposition may come from a source least expected. In Fairfax County, Virginia, in the metropolitan

Washington, DC, area that serves approximately 130,000 young people in its county public school district, a child care program that would serve teen parents was discussed. Plans were abandoned when a local PTA opposed the program, feeling it would encourage teens to have babies. The phrase, "Don't make assumptions," is an apt one here.

Community groups that should be supportive of prevention or care programs still need to be educated about issues, and their support actively recruited.

Speaking Their Language

When you present your case to key decision-makers and groups within your community, it is important to know your audience and tailor your presentation to the group's particular interests and issues. Have someone with credibility in the particular group make the presentation. S/he will speak the language of the audience.

People and groups usually do things which they perceive to be in their best interest. By linking the identified need and the program idea to the interests of the individual group, you will be more likely to gain the support of that group.

If you present your case to a group of medical professionals, you want to stress the health implications of the program. If you talk with educators, you want to emphasize the need to keep young people in school.

If you're talking with representatives from the business and corporate sector, you want to highlight the need to keep young people in school to give them critical job skills.

Service clubs may be interested in ways programs for teens can help reduce the chances that young people will be involved in at-risk behaviors. And in all cases, it is best if you can find a respected leader from that profession or organization to present your case.

Support Through Awareness Campaign

Marie Mitchell, co-author of the **Postponing Sexual Involvement Curriculum, Grady Memorial Hospital, Atlanta, Georgia,** credits their initial Community Awareness campaign

in 1980 for the lack of negative reactions to the PSI program
developed for middle school students.

Grady Memorial Hospital staff recognized the need for teen
pregnancy prevention. They decided to go to the community for
input on the most-needed services. Atlanta's Coalition on
Responsible Parenthood, a coalition of thirty-seven community
agencies, was formed. Atlanta Mayor Maynard Jackson and his
wife agreed to co-chair the Awareness Campaign.

A twelve-minute trigger film was produced which presented
the statistics and the problems of adolescent pregnancy in the
area. In the film, Atlanta leaders, including the mayor, superintendent of schools, a local minister, and a businessperson,
discussed the subject.

A discussion manual was prepared to accompany the film.
Bumper stickers, flyers, and other promotional materials were
also prepared for distribution.

Each of the thirty-seven agencies participating in the Coalition agreed to provide volunteer facilitators from within their
own agencies who were then trained to go into the community
and lead discussion groups. Several hundred group meetings
were held, and at each one, participants were asked to complete
a survey which asked how they wanted to work on the teen
pregnancy issue. Mitchell commented:

> *The consensus of the community was that primary
> efforts should be devoted to assisting young people in
> postponing early sexual involvement. Therefore, we really
> didn't have negative reactions for this program because it
> grew out of a community awareness campaign.*
>
> *As a health agency, we're actually carrying out a
> community mandate. And that's one way of cutting down
> on resistance—have the community look at the problem
> and be a part of developing the solution.*
>
> *The Atlanta Superintendent of Schools, as part of his
> commitment to our Awareness Campaign, agreed to help
> with whatever the community wanted. He followed
> through by allowing us to implement our PSI program
> throughout the Atlanta school system.*

Working Through Community Catalyst

When you're looking for a person or persons to serve in the visible public leadership position, it's advisable to recruit a "Community Catalyst." The Community Catalyst is a person, or in some cases a group, who is well-known, well-connected, well-respected, and has clear credibility in the community. Direct service providers certainly have credibility in their field and in the community. But when it comes to the type of credibility with the clout and the connections to make things happen, successful programs often solicit help from a key community member to serve as the lead figure in the public arena.

The Community Catalyst is most often someone who is involved in a wide range of community activities, and is perhaps in a prominent community position. Community Catalysts have extensive networks which include members of the business sector and policy-makers.

"Are you willing to give it one more shot?
Go the rounds one more time?"

Program professionals can *identify* the people in the community's formal and informal power structure, but the Community Catalyst is someone who knows those individuals on a first-name basis, sees them at meetings and social events, and gets phone calls returned promptly. Also, service providers who take the lead public role may be seen as having a vested interest such as a paycheck, job security, or self-promotion. The Community Catalyst, on the other hand, is someone who gets no direct, tangible compensation for his/her involvement, but appears to be supporting the program for the general community good. That's important.

Marge Eliason, whose proposed parenting and child care program was lost because of negative reactions of some community people, tried again, this time with the help of a Community Catalyst. She reported:

> *A few months later I was sitting in my classroom*
> *feeling terrible that we had failed, that we wouldn't*

Young Families Program, Billings, MT
Play yard donated by community organizations.

have this program. But I still knew we had to have it. I called the school nurse who had worked with me and said, "Are you willing to give it one more shot? Go the rounds one more time?" She didn't want to, but she agreed we had to do it.

So we got our coffee and cookies ready and asked people to meet again. This time we targeted a woman in town, Judy Peterson from the Junior League. Judy is assertive, a mover and a shaker. We got her to buy into the concept, and we asked her to chair the whole thing. She was our Community Catalyst.

With Judy's leadership, we went to the hospital and asked for help. The hospital had bought up many homes in the area for future expansion. They decided to let us use one of their homes, and helped with the renovation needed to meet day care licensing standards.

This was the community's project,
and it was no longer popular to say
we were going to cause pregnancy.

We had been awarded several small grants, so now we had a site and a small amount of money.

We went back to the school board and asked if they would fund an instructor, instructional material, and class accreditation. They agreed, and we started in the fall of 1984 with nine students. We received our grant from the Office of Adolescent Pregnancy Programs (OAPP/DHHS) in September.

It's very important to let the community take ownership. This was their project, and it was no longer popular to say we were going to cause pregnancy. We had a lot of key people involved this time . . . an attorney, a pediatrician, an obstetrician, and a Junior League member. Once all these people were involved and said we needed the program, those negative people climbed back into the woodwork and we haven't heard from them since.

*It was a blessing we were not totally school-funded.
Our schools have been in a terrible financial crisis, and
we would have been one of the first to go when budget
cuts came. We're now in a new house—still provided by
Deaconess Medical Center—three times as large, a
$50,000 commitment made by them. We now have
twenty-one babies and toddlers, thirty-two students, and
when school cuts are made, Young Families is not
threatened by the cutbacks.*

*The community helped paint, clean, and scrub our
way into our new facility, and they take a lot of personal
pride in the program.*

Involving Teens

As you gather support and present your case in the community, it is important continually to enlist the help of people from
different parts of the community including teens. Comments in
public meetings by articulate teen parents about the difficulties
they face have been crucial in convincing communities of the
need for services.

Too often adults plan programs for teens without any input
from the teens themselves. They know how they wish teens
would feel, think, and behave. However, it's been a while since
many of us have been teens, and the world has changed greatly.
It is important to get input from teens as needs are identified and
programs are planned. This will help build a broad base of
ownership in the effort from the beginning which will be a
valuable resource as programs are planned and implemented.

The Adolescent Single Parent Program at **Bowie High
School** in **Landover, Maryland,** is a good example of getting
teen input at the beginning. Their program was developed by a
group of home economics teachers who were concerned with
adolescent pregnancy, and also were experienced in parent
education. Their initial goal was to establish a pilot program that
would keep pregnant and parenting students in school.

In gathering data and developing the program idea, the staff
interviewed all of the teen mothers at the three area high schools
to determine the students' needs and the most effective way to

meet those needs. Agnes Kuhn, a teacher in the program, explained:

> *The extensive interviewing of all teen mothers in our community high schools gave us a clear understanding of the students' real life situations and needs. After we gathered our information from student interviews and other sources, we wrote a proposal and submitted it with the data to our County and State Boards of Education, and to key people in the Department of Health and Department of Social Services. Our supervisor walked the idea through several layers of administration, building support with key people along the way.*
>
> *Once the pilot program was established, we invited board of education members, representatives from the Governor's Office, health department officials, and local newspaper reporters to visit. This helped them become advocates for the program.*

Prevention Through Collaboration

The **Mecklenburg Council on Adolescent Pregnancy (MCAP)** in **Charlotte, North Carolina,** is an example of a successful teen pregnancy prevention, community collaboration effort. Since its inception in 1980, the Council has created pilot projects aimed at primary prevention. MCAP's prevention model encourages local organizations to address the problem of teenage pregnancy from their most effective vantage point and their philosophical perspective. The initial activities of the Council were chosen by the original task force leaders, and included a financial study, collection and mapping of adolescent pregnancy data in the entire county, a Teen Hot Line, a media awareness breakfast, and a local fact sheet. From that point, local prevention activities have expanded significantly to include, among others, such innovative programs as:

- Junior high school health fairs
- An "I'm an Askable Doc" project involving physicians in the community
- "It's OK to Say 'No!'" campaign during prom time

- Distribution of "TeenHelp" referral cards
- A prime-time, one-hour commercial-free, live "Talk to Your Kids" Sexuality Telethon featuring a panel of experts with a teen audience
- Workshops for clergy on sexuality education in the religious setting
- Workshops on adolescent health/legal issues

One of the most successful prevention activities sponsored by the MCAP is "Let's Talk" Month every October. The "Let's Talk" Month has grown over the past several years until it now includes a full month-long agenda of activities designed for parents, to provide information, and to encourage communication on sexuality with their children. The main goal of the "Let's Talk" prevention program is to help parents become "askable" parents.

Ideas to Action

It's important to remember that "Every community has the same cast of characters."

Whether a large metropolitan area or a rural area, every community has sources of data and information, service providers and community volunteers willing to gather the facts, and community catalyst facilitators who can begin to make things happen through their contacts and networks.

Thorough knowledge of your own community is the logical first step before launching into a new program. At this point, program options begin to take shape, and you start to define the strategies and program responses which will address the identified needs.

But beware of "paralysis by analysis." Some communities have wonderful reports that have done little except collect dust on an office shelf. Sooner or later, that *second* step must be taken if the needs of young people are to be served.

This is the point where you begin moving from the idea stage to ACTION!

Moving Into Action

The axiom, "Failure to plan means planning to fail," readily applies to many programs along the adolescent pregnancy prevention continuum. Planning is essential to the development of an effective program that carries out its stated mission. Good planning is important to secure adequate program funding.

Planning is a creative process that involves mapping out a course of action that will lead a program to its desired outcomes. Planning is an ongoing process that involves looking at how a program will operate and what its role will be within the community. Planning is perhaps the most critical part of effective program management.

The Planning Process

A program plan describes what you're going to do and how you'll generate the needed support to accomplish it. Developing a program plan involves looking at a number of factors:

- **Internal program environment**—what is needed to create an effective operation?
- **External community environment**—how will it impact the program?
- **Future environment in the community**—what will it mean for the program and its target population?
- **Trends**—what are the patterns and their implications for the program and its participants?
- **Barriers**—what are the potential barriers to the program, and how can those be minimized?
- **Resources**—what resources are available to implement a program, such as leadership, facility, management, funding, and equipment?

To begin planning an adolescent pregnancy program, start by establishing a core planning group. The planning group may include individuals involved in the needs assessment and information gathering. It may include individuals representing a particular expertise related to the subject matter or the client population. It needs to involve representatives from a cross section of the community—the schools, businesses, volunteer and civic groups, youth-serving agencies, medical professionals, media, local governmental agencies, and other key groups.

The initial planning group needs to be small enough to get things moving, but large enough to be truly representative of the values and resources in the community. It is best to have representatives from each segment of the community on the planning group who can speak on behalf of the groups represented, and obtain the necessary commitments.

If a program is to serve a particular client group, such as teens or pre-teens, it is important to secure input from representatives of that group during the planning phase. Too often, adults plan programs for teens that are based on adult needs, the adult's *perception* of the needs of young people, or factors that motivate adults, as opposed to the needs and issues relevant to teens or pre-teens.

Diverse representation is important. Many times, planning groups limit their focus and their access to potential resources by keeping their group's membership too homogeneous. If a

program is to serve the community, its chances for success will
increase if various segments of the community are involved in
the planning.

The value of having a diversity of people participate in the
program planning can't be overemphasized. Each different
group brings its own expertise, network of contacts, and access
to needed resources. For example, Richard Brookman, member
of the Committee on Adolescence, American Academy of
Pediatrics, recommends including a physician in any planning
related to adolescent health issues. Dr. Brookman said:

> *A physician may be the community's most respected
> authority on the medical facts of teenage pregnancy,
> pregnancy prevention, and associated problems such as
> drug use, infections, and nutrition.*
>
> *It's important to find a doctor who realistically accepts
> the fact that some teenagers are sexually active and can't
> be persuaded to be abstinent until marriage. Some physi-
> cians let their personal religious beliefs cloud their
> responsibility to provide accurate information to the
> community, to parents, or to individual young patients.*

Setting the Ground Rules

The planning group needs to identify its leadership and
methodology at the beginning of the planning process. Who is in
charge of directing the planning process and moving it forward?
What is the time frame involved? If a diversity of opinions is
represented on the planning committee, how will conflicts be
managed and resolved?

What is the structure of the planning group? Are they an
independent entity, or will they be preparing a final plan for
approval by some other board or group? How will other people
be recruited to become involved in the program planning
process?

These are issues to discuss at the outset. The planning group
may be an officially designated committee or task force of
another group, such as an adolescent pregnancy task force
formed by the local Board of Education. If so, the board of the

parent group will set the parameters for the planning group's operation.

If the planning group has evolved from a group of interested people who may not formally be representing any particular organization or agency, they will need to spend time developing the guidelines that will govern the planning process. As they proceed, if some parts of the process appear to be inefficient in terms of time, communication of information, or some other area, the process can be altered as needed.

According to the YWCA of the USA's manual, *Program Planning in the YWCA* (no longer in print), establishing clear ground rules in advance can help manage the resolution of conflicts when differences of opinion do occur—as they will. Suggested ground rules include:

- Focus on the issues, not personalities; depersonalize the situation as much as possible.
- Keep the lines of communication open and maintain discussion.
- Act in good faith, democratically, and with fairness; take it for granted that others are doing the same.
- Try to look inside the other person's (or group's) frame of reference.
- Emphasize common concerns and points of agreement.
- Avoid rigid positions, anger, and irritation.
- Seek creative alternatives that will meet the needs of both parties.

Is There an Ideal Program Model?

Is there one ideal model for prevention or care programs? Probably not. The programs being planned across the country offer a rich diversity of approaches to meet the needs in individual communities. That is as it should be, given the unique character of each community. When a community feels it has analyzed its own situation, developed a plan to grapple with its problems, and implemented its *own* plan, there is a sense of ownership, commitment, and local control that benefits the teens, teen parents, their children, parents, and the community at large.

However, some common factors are associated with successful local adolescent pregnancy prevention and care programs:

Programs must have **clear goals.**

They must have **adequate resources** to meet those goals and to maintain services. This is often the most difficult challenge of prevention and care programs. New programs may find start-up resources but have trouble maintaining and expanding resources over time. Once a program has passed its initial demonstration phase and has a documented track record of success, the program needs to develop permanent sources of funding.

Critical resources include funds, staff, and facilities plus a variety of health, education, and social services. In doing the initial community assessment and program planning, the availability of all these items must be carefully evaluated.

Obtaining resources usually means gaining **local public and political support.** Adolescent sexuality and pregnancy is a topic many people prefer to ignore. Most successful programs have had to deal in some way with many misconceptions. They have shown policy-makers and the public that resources directed to support prevention and care programs are a cost-effective investment for the community.

Successful programs put energy into **long-range planning** from the beginning. This means focusing on the type and amount of resources needed over time to build and maintain a program. To do otherwise is to invite management by crisis when the initial start-up period is over, a situation all too common.

Effective leadership and competent program management are no less important than resources. Many managers are the true, unsung heroes of successful (and struggling) programs. They are community organizers, promoters, trouble-shooters, fundraisers, client recruiters, politicians, and magicians.

Some programs may appear to have developed due to the efforts of one dynamic and high-profile individual. However, successful programs aren't built and sustained over the years through the efforts of a single person, no matter how charismatic and motivational. It takes a coordinated community commitment

to create a successful program. Strong leadership, both employed staff and volunteer, makes that coordination possible.

It is not enough simply to assume that things are working
because kids are in the program, the staff is committed, there are
funds, and the community likes the program. Programs which
have well-coordinated, comprehensive services must include
evaluation as an important part of their overall operation. When
planning your program, don't forget that an evaluation process
needs to be part of the initial comprehensive plan.

The Vision Becomes the Mission

Once the problem has been identified, the program need
determined, appropriate information gathered, and the planning
committee established, a starting place in developing a specific
program is to transform the vision into a mission statement. The
mission statement is the ideal scenario, the ultimate desired
outcome. The mission statement defines the reason for the
program's existence and becomes its statement of purpose.

*The mission statement should be positive,
consensus-building, concise, and descriptive.*

The mission statement provides the overall guiding force for
the program. Goals, objectives, and activities are designed to
help the program carry out its mission and achieve its purpose.

The mission statement should be positive, consensus-
building, concise, and descriptive. It is not the place for lengthy
prose or words that send the reader running for the dictionary for
an interpretation. The mission statement of a program should
clearly state, "This is what we are and what we are about."

**Medina Children's Services Teenage Parent Program,
Seattle, Washington,** is a teenage pregnancy and parenting
interagency program providing comprehensive services through
collaborative partnership. It's mission statement is:

*To develop a comprehensive support system and
referral mechanism for all pregnant adolescents and/or
parents within the Seattle School District.*

Setting Goals and Objectives

When the general mission statement is developed, the planning group next needs to define the goals and objectives of the program. These determine what must be done to move the program toward the accomplishment of its mission.

Specific definitions of goals and objectives will vary somewhat. Primarily, goals are future-oriented, measurable, and relate to obtaining resources and achieving results. Goals describe broad future results, reflect the program's mission, and give direction for the objectives and program action. Goals do not usually have time constraints.

The goals of the Medina TAPP program include:

1) To promote positive parenting methods through parenting education.

2) To promote self-sufficiency and development of positive self-esteem.

3) To reduce incidence of child abuse within this specific population.

4) To provide comprehensive preventive services to address youth-at-risk of initial pregnancy and/or repeat pregnancy.

Objectives are more detailed statements of what must be done, by whom, and when to move toward the accomplishment of a particular goal.

Objectives are measurable and have specific targets, assignments of responsibility, and timetables. One objective for the second goal above could be:

1) To provide a weekly parenting support session for fifty teen parents that includes child development, nutrition, and other related information.

Action steps are the activities or events that will be implemented to achieve the objectives. The action steps are specific descriptions of exactly what will be done and by what dates. Action steps for the above objective for 1989 are:

1) Program staff will provide two-hour sessions Monday and Wednesday evenings for teen parents and their children at the Medina Center.

2) Child care and transportation will be provided for the participants by TAPP program volunteers.

Considering the Structure

How the program will be structured is an important part of the overall program plan. Will the program be part of an existing organization or institution such as the YWCA or school system?

Will the administration, funding, staffing, facility, supplies and other essential program components be provided by the administering organization? Or will the program be responsible for obtaining those items on its own?

If a program idea develops outside an existing entity, the planning group may consider whether it is more effective to link with an existing organization or to establish a new, autonomous program.

If the program becomes part of an existing organization, the roles, responsibilities, and lines of accountability need to be well defined in the planning stage.

When the program is set up as a totally independent operation, the planning group needs to consider a variety of organizational issues.

In her booklet, "The Buck Stops Here," Kathleen Fojtik, Associate Director of the **Student-Parent Center, Ann Arbor, Michigan,** outlined the following issues that need to be addressed by new non-profit programs:

- **Incorporation.** Will the program need to be incorporated to establish a legal entity through which to receive funds? The not-for-profit division of the agency in your state that handles incorporation issues will be able to assist you in completing this process. (Incidentally, the process of incorporation is much easier to accomplish in some states than in others.)
- **Selecting a Name and Corporate Seal (Logo).** This sounds like a simple task. What you are called, however,

is important, and choosing a name may actually be a difficult task. A name shouldn't be too cumbersome to say on the telephone or to fit on your letterhead. If an acronym is to be used, it helps if it's catchy or easy to pronounce. Once Articles of Incorporation are filed, the corporate name is set legally. Fojtik's advice is to choose a short and simple name that your program can live with over time. The logo is also important. It needs to look professional and serve the purpose of identifying your program. Be careful that neither your name nor your logo suggest either cultural or sex bias. For example, if you plan to serve both men and women, your name should reflect this goal.

- **Constitution.** This is the basic statement of general purpose and principles by which an organization is formed and administered.
- **Bylaws.** Bylaws are exactly that—the laws by which an organization operates, the rules of your corporation. All basic procedural rules should be found in the bylaws. Bylaws can be changed and amended from time to time, but need to provide a firm operational framework. With good bylaws, everyone knows the rules and has a fair opportunity to interact within the basic structure.

At a minimum, bylaws should include the following:

Statement of Purpose. This will probably be the mission statement of the organization.

Name of the Corporation. The legal name that was given to the program when it was incorporated.

Membership Requirements. Programs may or may not be membership-based.

Dues/Membership Eligibility. If a membership-based program, dues and eligibility need to be defined.

Voting Rights. Who is eligible to vote, how, when, for whom?

Special and Regular Meetings. Regularly scheduled and special meetings are important to the on-going operation of a program. The bylaws should outline the frequency of meetings for the board and, if appropriate, the membership.

Quorum Requirements. What type of quorum is needed for action by the decision-making body?

Board of Directors. Every organization needs a working decision-making group to guide the organization. The bylaws should define the selection process and terms of office, the duties and responsibilities, meetings, and procedures.

Officers. President, Vice President, Secretary, and Treasurer are the traditional officers of most organizations. The bylaws should state the officer positions, the number, and their duties and responsibilities.

Committee Structure. The standing committees should be identified, as well as the process for establishing special ad hoc committees.

Amendment Process. The procedure for making changes to the bylaws should be clearly defined.

Dissolution Clause. This is legally required for bylaws of a non-profit, tax exempt organization. Standard language available for writing this section should be carefully followed.

You may want to ask the executive director of a well-organized group to review your bylaws.

- **Tax-exempt status.** A ruling by the Internal Revenue Service related to 501(c)(3) non-profit, tax-exempt status is important for any program wishing to receive funds from the United Way, private foundations, and/or from most government agencies. File for 501(c)(3) status as soon as possible. It can take several months to obtain. Contact your nearest IRS office for the appropriate forms. Also request the form to apply for an Employer Identification Number. This is also important, and should accompany your IRS application. Once your program has received non-profit, tax-exempt status, you will need to file an annual IRS report on Form 990. This is the return to be submitted by organizations exempt from federal income tax.
- **Internal Personnel Policies.** This procedure can be simple at first if staffing for the program is small, and can be expanded over time as the program grows.

Putting the Pieces Together

When a program plan is completed, you may want to get some feedback from key people outside the planning group. They can help you review the plan from different perspectives. Talking with potential funding sources in the community will be helpful in finalizing the goals of the program plan.

When planning adolescent pregnancy prevention or care programs, remember for whom the program is designed. Successful programs must identify, recruit, and serve the adolescents most at risk in the community, be it for too-early sexual involvement, pregnancy, or parenthood. However, this is not as easy as it may seem on paper. Teens are a challenging group under the best of circumstances. Add multi-ethnic communities, poverty, school failure, special-needs youth, and the developmental tasks which adolescents experience, and the challenges become extreme.

Myra Nash Johnson, Director, **Arts of Living Institute, Catholic Charities, Chicago, Illinois,** stressed the need first to understand your target community's culture and to be involved in that community. She said:

> *You have to know the community, and cultural sensitivity isn't enough—you also have to know where McDonald's is. That means a long-term commitment to the community.*
>
> *You don't go straight to the school and say, "I have this wonderful pregnancy prevention program for you." You have to establish relationships first, build the respect of the community including the professionals—public aid, health people, school people.*
>
> *They need to see you at PTA meetings and know you're an interested participant. Community residents need to hear you talk about this teen pregnancy issue in their churches. This is what we did. Somebody talked with the churches, someone with the schools. It's active participation. It's optimal to hire from the community. If you can't, you need to do even more trust-building within that community.*

*If you do hire from the community, you and your
agency must make a long-term commitment to professional training and skills building. We're talking about an
impoverished community. If you hire residents, you can
have a staff that reflects the composition of the community. There will be a connectedness you simply can't get
otherwise.*

Johnson also emphasized the importance of respecting clients
and the strengths of their families. She continued:

*We work from a position of strength, not weakness. We
don't look at our clients and focus on drug use and other
negatives. Instead, we see how strong our families are to
have withstood these things all these years. Our role is to
facilitate their growth.*

*We want the family to grow positively, but we don't put
judgments on what positive means. Relationship is always
the key.*

Mary Hughes, Vice President for Community Services,
National March of Dimes Birth Defects Foundation,
addressed the same issue:

*We're just now beginning to realize how important it is
for an organization to be credible to a community, especially in a community at risk. How can you be an appropriate messenger if you haven't walked in somebody
else's shoes?*

*I think we need to be giving grants to put a resource
mother in the community to talk with young women and
shepherd them through the system. I think this is just as
necessary as putting a social worker in an adolescent
pregnancy clinic. We need to funnel resources into
community people to handle problems. It's a matter of
where you put your shrinking dollars, and I think we need
to empower people in the community to solve their
problems.*

*Much of our funding continues in the area of prenatal
care, but we're spending a lot today to educate communities to the problem of lack of care. We're spending more
money on community education and on media campaigns
that are linked to services in the community.*

Listen to the Young

In planning a program, always remember the young people
you are serving. Listen to the words of Lina Johnson, a 1985
graduate of New Futures School, as quoted in *Our Troubled
Teens* (1987: Generation at Risk), page 34:

*I came to this school last year, a frightened little girl.
Today I am leaving as a young woman with strength and
wisdom, and ready to face anything that comes my way. I
thought my life was shattered forever. New Futures helped
put the pieces back together again and opened doors for
me. Not only did I receive a good academic education, but
a valuable education in parenting, health, nutrition, and
job training. Because of what I have received at New
Futures, I am a jump ahead. I only know that because of
you, faculty, staff and friends, I am prepared to face the
future and need not fear it. You all have given me the
chance to achieve my goals and follow my dreams.*

This is what local adolescent pregnancy prevention and care
programs are about—reaching young people who need support,
encouragement, and opportunities as they move through
adolescence to adulthood.

On the local level, programs have the opportunity to reach
young people in a caring, personal way. Overall, the quality of
the relationship between adult and teen may be the most
important variable to program success.

Respect, caring, and the personal connection makes the real
difference in adolescent pregnancy programs that are successful
in helping young people postpone early sexual activity, avoid
unplanned pregnancy, and counter the negative consequences of
too-early childbearing.

The time spent planning a program is time well spent. Talk with people to get their advice so you can learn from others' experience. Be realistic about what it will take to set up and operate a program—staff, facility, funding, outreach. Map it all out. What are the goals and objectives? How will they be carried out? By whom? How much will it cost and how long will it take?

Take time to plan—it's essential to the success of your program.

CHAPTER 6

Determining The Focus

Where a program idea is initiated will to some degree define what the program focus and content will be. As you explore the type of program to develop, look carefully at the continuum of prevention in these terms:

- **Target Population.** Who will be involved in the program—boys and/or girls, teens and/or pre-teens, siblings, parents, children of teen parents?
- **Specific Intervention Strategy.** What type of service or activity is appropriate to achieve the goals and to reach the target population?
- **Method.** How will the service intervention be planned, delivered, and evaluated?
- **Location.** Where is it most appropriate for the program to be located to serve the target population most effectively?

Depending on defined needs, available resources, and community priorities, any starting place on the prevention continuum is all right. Just don't lose sight of the big picture.

A program that starts with job training for youth may run into
high school dropouts who are also parents. Until child care,
housing, and parenting responsibilities are met, no vocational
program will succeed with this population.

A program which focuses on adequate prenatal care for
pregnant teens may soon find itself enmeshed in preventive
education before the fact of pregnancy. This is a common
experience. A continuous monitoring of all needs and resources
is required for a responsible coalition to build its comprehensive
approach.

Adolescent pregnancy prevention and care programs are
usually divided into three or four main categories based upon the
content of the information presented or the services delivered.
The big three categories are Health, Academic/Vocational, and
Social Services.

This discussion considers each of these categories in their
broadest context. Many prevention and care programs include
more than one category. Truly comprehensive programs offer all
three kinds of service, whether on site or through linkages.

Health Services Include Prevention and Care

Health programs may include:
- Physical and mental wellness for teen and pre-teen males
  and females
- Nutrition education
- Sexuality education
- Pre- and post-natal care
- Maternal and infant care
- Family planning.

The Hub—Center for Change for South Bronx Teens is
an example of a comprehensive program which offers a range of
health and educational programs to teenagers to "help them stay
clear of the traps of too-early pregnancy, unfinished education,
drugs and violence so they can take charge of their own lives
and futures successfully," according to Mary Morales, Director/
Clinic Administrator.

Sponsored by Planned Parenthood of New York City, The
Hub provides a holistic approach to meeting the needs of

teenagers so they can find options other than early childbearing. In addition to providing prenatal and other services in the Reproductive Health Center, the staff runs a Parent Education Program (PEP), and outreach workers go into the school system with their Sexuality Education for Teens (SET) program.

The second component of The Hub is a group of educational, pre-vocational, and recreational programs based on the third floor of the Bronx Center. An open internal stairway links these activities with the second floor health services. Many younger teens come to The Hub specifically for these programs.

As in other areas, much of the unplanned pregnancy and childbearing among teens in this community is linked to disappointment and failure in school. The school dropout rate in the South Bronx is seventy-five percent. All teens whose initial interview indicates some problem in school are referred to the Learning Center. Any teen who enters the Learning Center or Recreation program must have a comprehensive medical exam which includes family planning.

A peer tutoring component is offered at The Hub. Peer teachers are paid minimum wages and provide one-to-one and group tutoring. Computer training and an employment program is offered, seventeen weeks of intensive training which leads to a certificate of achievement.

School to Employment Progam (STEP) is for sixteen- to eighteen-year-olds who have left school. This is a thirteen-week course leading to a certificate which increases career opportunities. STEP also provides GED training, job awareness, interview skills, and other activities to prepare clients for the world of work. Pregnant young people are included in the STEP program.

Project Street Beat, based off site, is a program designed to provide concrete services and emotional support to young people, male and female, who are engaging or at risk of engaging in risky behavior such as teen prostitution and I.V. drug use, Morales explained.

An outreach team travels by van to designated areas in the Bronx. Emergency food, clothing, condom distribution, escort services for medical treatment, and AIDS education and risk reduction are a few of the services available.

"We developed these comprehensive services at The Hub because Planned Parenthood realized that providing birth control information is not enough. You need to reach the whole person rather than simply treating part of the problem. We provide young people with real alternatives to too-early child-bearing," Morales concluded.

The Youth Health Services of Elkins, West Virginia, offers comprehensive health services to pregnant and parenting adolescents and other high-risk teens within an almost three thousand square mile sparsely populated rural region of Appalachia. Program services are delivered in three outreach centers located within the designated region.

The agency has incorporated the Community of Caring values-oriented approach into its program services for four years, and has developed creative ways to provide support, education, and life skills training for the teens. The wide range of activities includes everything from health care to a gardening project that teaches nutrition. The latter brings teens in touch with their Appalachian cultural heritage which has a strong identification with the land.

Academic/Vocational Focus

Academic/Vocational programs may include:
- Dropout prevention
- Family life education
- Mainstream or alternative programs for high risk youth
- Academic and special classes for pregnant and parenting teens
- Targeted curricula
- Formal or informal educational activities
- Job skills training
- Career goals
- Child development
- Parenting education.

The **Cities in Schools** approach is a broad-based community/ school collaboration headed by Bill Milliken. Milliken uses a comprehensive, caring approach for youth at risk of failure, whether or not they are involved in too-early pregnancy and parenting. Almost twenty-five years ago he and his colleagues established his first Street Academy working with inner-city kids on Manhattan's Lower East Side. The program became successful in getting young dropouts into neighborhood alternative schools.

Sponsored by corporations from that beginning, the Street Academy concept evolved into the successful **Cities in Schools (CIS)** program. CIS brings the resources of the community into alternative and traditional school settings to serve the needs of at-risk youth. Currently CIS has more than 150 local dropout prevention programs in thirty-three cities throughout the United States. More than eighteen thousand at-risk youth and their families have been served by CIS programs this past year.

These programs generally are small with an emphasis on bonding between students and adults. Students get a heavy dose of counseling to help them cope with personal problems. Classroom instruction, which is often remedial, is combined with lessons aimed at preparing students for jobs.

---

*People are hungry
for a sense of community.*

CIS is about connecting the disconnected, according to Milliken. By "brokering" the various youth agencies and getting them to put their people and resources in the schools, CIS connects the fragmented and disconnected resources that various youth-serving agencies bring to the community. This bringing together of service providers at a single site provides teams of caring adults in close connection with small groupings of young people in a personal, accountable, and coordinated fashion, he said. Milliken continued to describe the Cities in Schools concept:

> *Not only are the children connected with the various resources they may need—from drug counseling to tutoring, from health care to job training—but to each other and their families. CIS has learned that when love goes where young people are and pays the price of*

*entering into their pain, their needs can be provided for
and a sense of hope can be imparted.*

*Adolescent pregnancy is not the problem. Literacy is
not the problem. Drugs are not the problem. The problem
is we have broken up our communities. People are hungry
for a sense of community.*

*We need education and we need medication, but that
alone won't solve the problems. Education is important,
awareness is important, but if you think you'll win this
battle for prevention of too-early pregnancy with education alone, you're going to lose. Education is a tool, it's
not the end result.*

*Relationships solve things. The issues are loneliness,
feelings of "Nobody cares," "I feel rotten," "I feel
unsafe," "Nobody knows I exist." The relational model is
most important. We have to have that love and that caring
both at the individual level and the corporate level.*

*The school is the best place to coordinate services for
young people. Over the years the school has become the
hub of the community. In many instances it has taken the
place of the extended family and of the religious community. In the school you can coordinate resources. The
teacher, the social worker and the health worker can
model working together, the process of brokering the
resources to kids rather than expecting the kids to run all
over town for services.*

*The whole idea of Cities in Schools is the creation of
public/private partnerships to bring existing public and
private human resources and services into the schools
where they can most benefit at-risk youth.*

A community interested in the CIS concept first needs the
backing of the school system. At the superintendent's invitation,
CIS/National will assist in the development of public/private
partnerships between the school system, local government,
public agencies, the private sector, and other community leaders.

A local Board of Directors, chaired by a representative from
the business sector, is developed to assess the community's

needs, leverage existing resources, and raise funds to support a CIS facilitation team. This team brings needed resources to at-risk youth through moving existing personnel from multiple programs onto a single education site.

Providing Employment Training

Building self-sufficiency skills through employment training and placement programs has become an increasingly important program piece in serving pregnant and parenting teens.

Barbara Cambridge, past president of the Texas Association Concerned with School Age Parenthood (TACSAP) and vice chair of the **Impact '88 Youth-at-Risk** committee in **Dallas**, says, "There have been many job-related programs for young people over the years. But to have a lasting impact, we need to make sure young people receive meaningful training for meaningful jobs."

Rich's Academy (Cities in Schools Program) is an alternative educational program for students who have dropped out or are at high-risk for dropping out of the Atlanta school system. The program is a cooperative venture between the Cities in Schools Program, the Atlanta public school system, Fulton County, and Rich's Department Store. Rich's provides the site for the program as well as some part-time employment opportunities.

Another program providing meaningful training as well as important support services is the **Expectant and Parenting Youth Program (EPYP)** operated by the **Lehigh Valley Private Industry Council (PIC), Allentown, Pennsylvania.** The program serves the highest-risk children referred by the Department of Social Services, schools, or probation officials.

EPYP is located in a huge building that houses all components of the PIC program. A nursery is adjacent to the classrooms, and the participants are responsible for feeding breakfast and lunch to their babies. The teen parents also participate in an early childhood development class once a week.

Health services, counseling, transportation, breakfast, and lunch are provided. Currently, funds are being raised to buy a house and provide residential services.

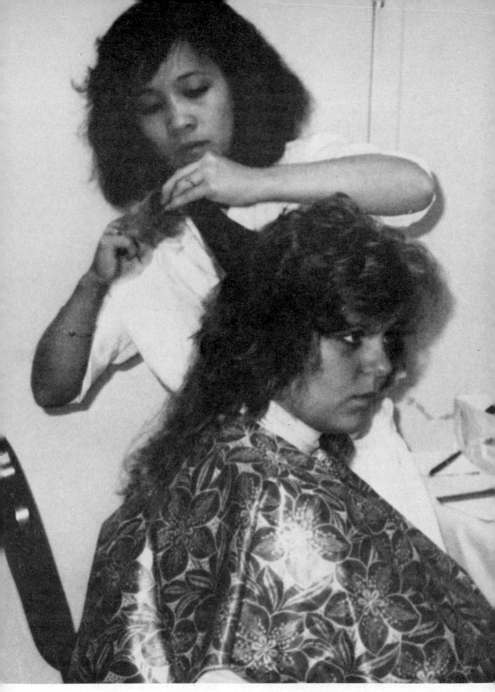

Voc/Tec Training, Washington State

Kathy Calabrese, Deputy Director of Day Care Operations, says, "To become self-sufficient, the basic needs of the pregnant and parenting teens must be met first. Along with the development of job skills, we focus on building self-esteem, confidence, and parenting skills. Giving the teens a sense of self-esteem and a feeling of being loved is essential to the success of this program."

An active, involved advisory council is critical, according to Calabrese. Bob Gombos, former chair of the Private Industry Council board and Vice President of Human Resource Development for Pennsylvania Power and Light, was an active advocate for the program. He helped initiate an emergency hotline so participants could call each other or a staff member if they faced a crisis situation. He commented:

I was invited to talk with the teens about the job market and careers. At the end of my talk, I asked if there were any questions. I got a lot of questions, but few of them were about jobs. I was one of the few males who had ever walked in the door to spend time with them, talk with them, and listen to them.

I go to the program every few weeks to be a facilitator for discussions with the participants. They share their concerns about all kinds of issues, especially those related to their day-to-day life. If you'd like to get representatives from the business community involved in social service programs, invite them to come and talk with the program participants, then leave the door open for further involvement.

Social Service Programs

Social Service/Life Skills programs may include:

- Counseling
- Self-esteem
- Decision-making
- Problem-solving activities
- Teen parent support activities—males and females
- Transportation

- Housing
- Child care
- Mentor programs
- Sibling or grandparent activities
- Male responsibility
- Self-sufficiency development
- Outreach.

The Ounce of Prevention Fund, founded in 1982, serves
Illinois' infants, children, teens, and their families, especially
families at-risk because of poverty and other factors that can
interfere with healthy child development.

Public money, funding community-based programs for
almost 100,000 Illinois residents, is enhanced by private contributions, which gives the Ounce the capacity critically to
evaluate its work and to try innovative approaches in services.

Thirty-seven **Parents Too Soon** programs are administered
by the Ounce of Prevention Fund and funded by Illinois' Department of Children and Family Services. More than 85,000 young
people have been involved in projects designed to prevent first
pregnancies, and eight thousand teen parents have received
support services.

Among many other projects administered by the Ounce is the
**Center for Successful Child Development (Beethoven
Project).** The Beethoven Project is operated by the Ounce in
conjunction with the Chicago Urban League. Families from six
buildings of the Robert Taylor Homes public housing development on Chicago's south side are participating in a demonstration program to provide continuous, comprehensive services to
children who will attend Beethoven Elementary School.

Services at CSCD include family advocates who make home
visits, a family drop-in center, Head Start, special programs for
teen mothers, and health care for pregnant women and their
young children.

The Ounce of Prevention Fund's program and research staff
monitor and evaluate programs on an on-going basis with the
goal of improving services for Illinois' at-risk children and their
families and adding to the knowledge in the fields of early
childhood and adolescence.

Our Place, developed by **Family Focus, Evanston, Illinois,** and funded in part through Ounce of Prevention, was started as a teen parent support center. "We came into prevention through the back door because kids were coming to our Center who weren't pregnant or parenting, and we didn't want to tell them not to come. That would have been like saying, 'Go get pregnant, then you can join us,'" explained Delores Holmes, Director of Our Place. She continued:

We began to think of ways we could have them in the Center, give them some information, and let them know there were other options besides getting pregnant. Now we have fifth through eighth graders in our prevention program, some of them siblings of our teenage mothers. We give them opportunities to look at a variety of things they can do and ways they can excel. We push education because we feel if they're successful in school, they'll be able to set goals and work toward them.

Usually the kids who come to the Center aren't the kids who get a chance to excel at the extracurricular activities at school. That's why we have a lot of events, prizes, dances, cultural experiences.

Kids need to try out ideas on adults. They need to get feedback that's honest and straightforward but not prudish. This little girl says, "He starts rubbing me and I feel all excited."

We say, "That's a very normal feeling, but you can't let it get out of control." We have to let them know that if they're sexually active, they certainly need to be responsible. We stress that the best contraceptive is saying "No," but the reality is that some of them are sexually involved.

We have a lot of one-on-one counseling. We're trying to help kids not to be anything less than successful, to plan, to dream . . .

Holmes stressed the need for community involvement through volunteers who can donate money, materials, and time.

Perhaps the most important tactic is to invite community people
to visit the program. "Once they see us, they're sold," she
observed.

Volunteers as Mentors

While volunteers greatly enrich programs and speak to the
community's commitment to the challenges of adolescent
pregnancy and parenting, they must be working in partnership
with paid professionals. As for all programs, volunteers must be
appropriately recruited, screened, trained, and supported. The
goals of the program must be clearly understood by the volunteer. The expectations for the role of the volunteer and the
expectations the volunteer has for the program must be clearly
articulated at the beginning. Volunteers who are well-matched to
a particular program's needs can be a valuable resource.

The Mentor Mother program was developed by the **Marion
County Extension Service, Indianapolis, Indiana,** to meet the
needs of pregnant and parenting teen moms. The goal of the
program is to enhance the self-esteem and knowledge of the teen
mom in order to have a positive impact upon her life goals and
her role as a parent.

This program uses a big sister approach and lots of volunteers. Each summer, adult mentors are recruited for the program.
Mentors are trained in September, and the program runs October
through June.

The program initially received a grant from the local March
of Dimes to develop training materials and purchase infant car
seats. The County Extension Homemakers Association and other
community organizations provided funds for snacks, door
prizes, and other small operational expenses.

The program was started by Janet Wakefield, 4-H Youth
Agent. Since that time, the program has grown to include a
Child Abuse Prevention grant which helped fund two to three
part-time staff members. Other grants have helped support
various activities.

Currently, the program is directed by Jane Hildenbrand,
Marion County Extension Human Development Specialist. The
program is now taking on a community collaborative effort. Big

Sisters of Central Indiana will be administering and directing the program, pending grant approval. The Extension Service will provide training for staff, mentors, and teens, and is developing new materials through the Home Economics Department. Christamore House, a community center, will be the host agency for the initial effort.

Building a Community-Wide Focus

The Horizon Youth Services of Harlingen, Texas, grew out of a local task force on reducing teen pregnancy, and provides a list of prevention and care services for young people in the South Texas community. Prevention services are fully bilingual, and include a twenty-four-hour information and referral hotline, family life education in the middle and senior high schools, peer counseling groups, and individual and group counseling.

The Horizon Youth Services sponsors a number of special events designed to increase community awareness. These include a Teen Awareness Day which involves skits, discussion groups, a health fair, and many festive "just for fun" activities. The program uses a large number of volunteers and enjoys strong community support.

Key elements related to the program's success are a strong referral network, a wide range of services, and acceptance by the community—especially teenagers—as a non-threatening, accessible entry point for counseling and education.

"We do education and counseling because any counseling agency worth its salt has to educate," commented Margo Jaenike, Director, Horizon Youth Services Center, "We can't put blinders on. But we're neutral in terms of the abortion issue, and also with birth control. Because of our neutrality, we have maintained a good relationship with the community."

Working Toward Comprehensive Services

Whether you're working from a health, education, or social service standpoint, you can often work toward more comprehensive services by linking formally or informally with programs providing other types of services for the same target population.

An individual never has only health, only education, or only social service needs. An effective program looks for ways to coordinate the health, education, and social service components so that each client receives the full range of services s/he needs. This doesn't mean one program must provide them all. It does mean that some system should be developed to ensure that the young people don't fall through the cracks in the service delivery system.

A wide variety of programs are in operation. Yours should be uniquely suited to the needs of your community, but on the other hand, don't reinvent the wheel. In these chapters you may find a model for achieving your goal of developing an adolescent pregnancy prevention or care program. Adapt that model to the needs of the young people in your area, making sure you have the content and focus you need to meet your program goals.

CHAPTER 7

Considering Program Setting

Adolescent pregnancy prevention and care programs are operating in a wide variety of settings across the country. Factors such as budget restrictions, the location of the organization administering the program, the availability of donated or shared space, the need to be near other programs serving the target population, the desire for either high or low visibility, or the accessibility to public transportation all go into determining the specific location for a program.

Variety of Settings

The Young Parent's Education Center, Great Falls, Montana, started in the basement of a church because it offered space, availability, and convenience. The program provides child care for teen moms; counseling, referral, and outreach services for teen parents; and teen parent panels for the eighth through tenth grade Family Living classes in the local schools.

In **Chico, California,** the **Pregnant Minor/Teen Parenting Program** started in a converted classroom at a continuation high school because it was the only space available at the time—a fairly common reason given for the selection of the first location for many programs.

The **Pregnant Minor Program, Redding, California,** began in 1968 in a teacher's home because, according to lead teacher Barbara Davis, "There was nowhere else to go."

The **Lawndale Family Focus Program in Chicago** started in a renovated store-front setting where "the rent was the lowest."

The **Adolescent Health Center of Terry Reilly Health Services, Nampa, Idaho,** started in a low-rent house on the main street of town.

Prevention programs like the **Postponing Sexual Involvement Educational Series** have been offered in settings from school classrooms to churches to community centers in housing projects.

Teens 'N Touch is an **Urban League** pregnancy prevention program which operates in two high-density public housing sites in **Charlotte, North Carolina.** In each housing project, the City of Charlotte Housing Authority has provided an apartment for Teens 'N Touch. Donald Bowan, Vice President, Programs, explained:

> *We've converted these apartments into learning centers. Two staff members, a health educator and an education specialist, divide their time between the two centers. We provide lots of tutoring with the help of volunteers.*
>
> *Sometimes it's a little difficult to recruit volunteers to work in the housing project. Generally they're college students.*
>
> *Our main goals for the program are to reduce pregnancy and parenthood among teens living in public housing, and increase the percentage of those completing high school. Our evaluation shows we're achieving those goals.*

In selecting a location for an adolescent pregnancy prevention or care program, consider the geographic location within the boundaries of the area to be served, the location within the facility which will house the program, and the atmosphere of the specific space assigned for program use.

Choosing Geographic Location

Several questions need to be answered in determining an appropriate geographic location for the program.

- Is the location convenient for the teens who are to participate in the program? Is it close to where they live, work, or attend school?
- Will the teens be able to get to the program site at the times the program is being offered?
- Are other programs or services for teens located nearby which may supplement the program?
- Is public transportation available to this area from all parts of the community?
- Is this a part of the community where teens will feel comfortable and safe whether they come alone or with friends?
- Will you use volunteers? If so, is this an area with potential volunteer sources in the immediate neighborhood? Is the area familiar to volunteers from other parts of the community? Is there parking or bus service nearby?

To reach a greater number of their potential clients, the **Maternal Health Center, Bettendorf, Iowa,** followed the trend of some health facilities in California by moving their maternal and child health location into a new shopping mall. Now pre- and postnatal check-ups for the teens in their program are located in a setting that is visible and familiar to the teens. Tom Fedje, Director, explained:

We moved here a few years ago, and I'm convinced this is the way to go. Young people hang out at the shopping mall, so we decided our program should be where they naturally spend their time. We're also accessible with more bus routes to the mall than almost any other place in town, and we have plenty of parking.

Besides, if an obstetrician has to leave to do a delivery,
the patient can kill time here at the shopping mall while
she's waiting.

Is It Teen Oriented?

Additional questions need to be considered when analyzing
the specific facility for the program.

- Is the exterior of the facility welcoming and attractive for
  teens? This doesn't mean new and expensive. But is there
  an easily identifiable entrance area that at least indicates to
  the teens that they are in the right spot, and that they are
  welcome?
- Is the entrance easily identifiable from the parking area or
  public transportation area?
- If the teens will be involved in the program during the
  evenings or late winter afternoons, is the entrance area well
  lighted and safe after dark?
- If the program is located in a facility where a number of
  other activities occur, is there a quick, easy, and unintimi-
  dating way for the teens to find the program upon entering
  the facility?
- Does the first impression upon entering give the feeling
  that this is a caring, welcoming, and friendly place?
- Are young people readily visible upon entering the facility? Teens attract teens! At the time in their lives when
  peers are most important, it is essential that teens entering
  the program facility for the first time see other young
  people already involved in the activities.

Ann Sandven, project director of **CONNECT,** a case management oriented program for pregnant and parenting teens in
rural Idaho, describes their health clinic:

We're in an old house, small, with two bedrooms. I
think teens need an environment that's more personal
instead of a big clinic where they can get lost in the
system. The teen clinic is small and cozy. The waiting
room is the living room, and the nurses's station is in
the kitchen.

We catch everybody because we're all there. It's not intimidating because we don't have older women there with their husbands (although about one-third of our patients are either married or living together). We're quicker, and we have a TV to show videos.

We put pictures of clients, partners, and their new-born babies up. We also have an adoption corner with pictures of adoptive families along with the brochures.

Kids keep their appointments here better than they do at regular clinics.

Designing the Atmosphere

Finally, the atmosphere of the program space needs to be teen-oriented. Often a youthful atmosphere can be inexpensively created in any type of setting with posters, bulletin boards, bright colors, and teen accessories such as magazines, the sports section of the newspaper, local school activity flyers, and school newspapers.

In some programs, the teen participants are actively involved in designing and decorating their program setting. Helping to plan the look of their program space and to keep the space up is a way of providing problem-solving, decision-making, and self-esteem building activities outside of the program's formal curriculum content.

Just as the adults who are planning and administering the program need ownership, it is equally important that the teen participants develop ownership in the program. Creating the feeling that the program location is their space helps build that ownership.

Andre Watson, director of the **Male Youth Project** sponsored by the **Shiloh Baptist Church** in **Washington, D.C.**, said, "When someone enters our program area, there is no doubt that this is a place for kids. If this place didn't feel right," he continued, "they (teen and pre-teen males) wouldn't be here."

A good way to evaluate the atmosphere of the program space is to get feedback directly from teens.

• Does the area look like a place teens would want to come and to spend time?

- Is it readily apparent that the program space is designed to serve teens? Is the area attractive and welcoming? (Again, that doesn't mean new and expensive.)
- If teens will be there over meal times or after school, is food available in the immediate vicinity? (Preferably food options other than junk food.)
- Is the program space easy to clean and maintain?
- Are the furnishings appropriate and easy to clean and maintain?
- If a prevention program, do the messages on the posters and bulletin boards reinforce the goals of the program?
- If it includes a care program, are there appropriate, relevant materials and support services available for the pregnant and parenting teens and their children? Books and magazines on pregnancy and parenting need to be appropriate for teen parents. Child care needs to be provided nearby or the facility needs a child-proof area with cribs and toys, an area for diaper disposal, a storage place for diaper bags, and a refrigerator for bottles and toddler snacks. Employment information should be readily available.
- Do signs and posters state rules, procedures, and suggestions in positive ways, or do they contain a lot of "No" and "Don't" kinds of words?

The Teen Age Parent Program (TAPP), Louisville, Kentucky, was established in 1970 and has grown over the years into a nationally recognized comprehensive, well-coordinated, and successful school program model. TAPP provides services for about 500 pregnant and parenting students annually.

From the outside, the large brick structure looks like a typical old-style school building. Inside, however, the atmosphere radiates a warm and caring feeling. The floors and woodwork shine, the kitchen staff prepares meals that would rival a good restaurant, and the teaching facility demonstrates a strong commitment to professionalism combined with a deep empathy for the students.

Georgia Chaffee, TAPP Principal, says, "We love the building because it's so light and has such warmth. Pregnancy can be depressing enough for a young person, and we want the facility to be cheerful and bright."

Upon touring the building, a visitor said, "The word that comes to mind here is 'pride.' The principal is proud of the staff, the students, the facility, and the program, and that same pride is reflected by the staff and by the students themselves."

Prevention Programs in Schools

School can be a natural setting for programs anywhere on the prevention continuum—both adolescent pregnancy prevention and care programs. That's where a majority of the young people are, so recruitment is less difficult. The teachers are trained professionals experienced in working with adolescents. However, they will need special training and support in presenting information related to sexuality issues.

The Urban Middle Schools Adolescent Pregnancy Prevention Program (UMSAPPP) was started in 1985 with support from the Carnegie and Ford Foundations and administered through the **Academy for Educational Development.** Eight school districts in seven states have implemented pregnancy prevention activities in their middle schools.

UMSAPPP's work is based on the assumption that schools must play a key role in adolescent pregnancy prevention. They feel that middle school is the appropriate point of intervention for such activities. Collaboration with community agencies with a similar mission to serve at-risk youth is stressed.

School districts with UMSAPPP include Atlanta, Georgia; Boston, Massachusetts; Detroit, Michigan; Kansas City, Missouri; Los Angeles, California; Milwaukee, Wisconsin; Norfolk, Virginia; and Oakland, California.

The program emphasizes a life options approach linking teen pregnancy prevention and other school efforts to improved student skills, self-esteem, career orientation, and ability to stay in school. The middle school prevention programs in the eight districts involve a variety of program components:

- Life planning/decision-making skills
- Family life/sex education curricula
- Staff development/teacher training in sexuality

- Health services
- Mentoring
- Reaching males
- Parent education
- Career emphasis
- After school resource centers
- Focus groups on sexuality and values
- Art, culture, and drama programs dealing with sexual responsibility themes

The eight-city UMSAPPP project provided pregnancy prevention programs and interventions at fifty-five middle schools, involving 9,119 students and 974 school staff during its first two years of operation. Broadly, the major impact was the legitimation of pregnancy prevention activities at the middle school level, according to Michele Cahill, Vice President and Director, School and Community Services, Academy for Educational Development (AED). AED prepared the documentation report for the program.

School Settings for Teen Parents

Schools often are the best location for comprehensive programs for pregnant and parenting teens, as long as the all-important health and social services and child care are provided along with education services. Important supplementary services such as transportation, meals, health care, and counseling are usually components of the existing school program.

However, many pregnant teens have negative images of schools, and may function and learn much better in an alternative school setting. Alternative schools can create environments which promote positive behavior change and more rapid maturation into adult responsibility. On the other hand, many pregnant teens will continue to do well in their comprehensive home school. Most need special services, and these can be provided through a program in the home school.

Alternative school settings use various types of facilities. For example, the **New Horizons Program, Burleson, Texas,** is housed in a portable building housing classrooms, a library, a fully-equipped kitchen, and cribs along the classroom wall for on-site child care. New Horizons, which has a comprehensive and individualized instructional format, is a cooperative program involving several small area school districts and one teacher.

The School-Age Parenting and Infant Development (SAPID) Program in California is state-funded. Sixty-one (1986-1987) school districts in California have SAPID programs. These are designed to encourage teenage parents to remain in school by providing child care on or near the school site, transportation for the young parents and their babies, and parenting education. The SAPID program is integrated into the regular school curriculum, generally at a comprehensive high school.

> *If teens and their families
> don't know about the program,
> they obviously won't participate.*

School settings need to be carefully considered. Since the school is a visible community entity funded by public moneys and whose policies and programs are overseen by an elected or appointed board, some issues become politically sensitive. That is especially true for programs which are related to adolescent sexuality or pregnancy.

The high profile program can attract opposition if the program is misunderstood. Remember, however, it is difficult to recruit participants who need the program and to recruit the funding needed if the program is invisible. If teens and their families don't know about the program, they obviously won't participate.

A popular strategy in implementing prevention and care programs is to associate adolescent pregnancy with other related issues that are less controversial. Therefore, the focus of school programs could be on promoting the overall goals and mission of the school system.

For example, of prime importance is the prevention of school dropouts, keeping young people in school to complete their education, and giving young people in the community the academic and life skills needed to achieve their potential.

Health Care Settings

When you're planning a location for a program somewhere on the adolescent pregnancy prevention continuum, consider the types of program settings currently available in the community. Many successful adolescent pregnancy care programs started in health facilities. Finding advocates in the medical community who have the social prominence, medical expertise, and access to the resources needed for credibility in the community can play a key role in securing the program location.

Successful prevention programs in health settings focus on the total wellness of the young person as a primary goal. They may also link the prevention of early sexual activity and pregnancy with the prevention of other at-risk behaviors such as substance abuse.

In selecting a program setting in a health care facility, remember that doctors' offices, clinics, and hospitals can be intimidating and frightening places for adults. For a teen or pre-teen, that feeling of intimidation or fear is magnified.

A health care setting may have fewer incentives and motivating factors for teens than does a school or a community center where they will be with their peers in a more social context. It is essential that programs serving teens in a health care facility give a great deal of creative thought to the location, the setting, and the atmosphere, or the best planned program may never achieve its potential.

Health care programs for pregnant and parenting teens are being offered in a diversity of settings from store-front rooms to large hospital complexes in metropolitan areas. To provide a loving, caring atmosphere in settings that by nature are more stark and sterile is especially important when providing programs for teens.

Fairbanks Health Center, a State of Alaska agency, has a specialized adolescent program located in a brightly decorated room designed to attract teens. Mary E. O'Bryan, whose expertise is adolescent sexuality, coordinates the clinic. She and Cathy Mikitka, **Fairbanks Counseling and Adoption** counselor, provide programs throughout the community on issues of adolescent sexuality.

The clinic waiting room has two big picture windows "to watch the sun come up." (During part of the year in Alaska, of course, the sun rises and sets during clinic hours.) The room is bright and sunny with colorful, comfortable furnishings and lots of green plants. Almost covering one wall is a large fabric-covered bulletin board with brightly colored fabric pockets holding eye-catching and easy-to-read pamphlets. Topics of the printed materials include subjects such as self-esteem, talking with your partner about sex, and how to talk to your parents.

Thursday is drop-in day for teens, and the room is filled with kids (forty-five to fifty each week) from 8 a.m. to 6 p.m., according to O'Bryan.

Community Settings

This type of setting is tremendously diverse, and may include a city or county agency, a social service organization, rented store-front space, a youth-serving agency, or a church. Adolescent pregnancy prevention and care programs across the country have used an extensive variety of innovative community settings for the delivery of their programs.

One example is the **YWCA of Fort Worth and Tarrant County, Texas,** which leases an unused fire station from the city for one dollar per year. Working with the community to raise the necessary funds to renovate the building, the YWCA provides teen parent support programs and child care for teen parents attending a nearby high school.

Another community program is **Family Focus/Our Place** which purchased a large, unused school building in **Evanston, Illinois.** They renovated it for a multi-purpose program center providing an extensive array of drop-in activities, workshops, classes, and services.

Major focus is on prevention and care services for teen and pre-teen youth. The facility includes a large, fully equipped kitchen with institutional-sized appliances, a gym, and an on-site child care center. Part of the facility is rented for office/program use by other community organizations.

Project PIECES (Parents, Industry and Educators Cooperate for Educational Success) was developed because

parents couldn't leave their jobs to attend parent/teacher conferences at school. Now the conferences are held in the mill where
the parents work.

The principal and guidance counselor at Newton-Conover
Middle School (North Carolina) and the Catawba County
Council on Adolescents organized PIECES with help from the
personnel director at Ridgeview Mills, Inc. Fifty-five employees
met in the mill with their children's counselors during the
program's first year of operation. Six guidance counselors met
with parents once monthly from November through May during
the parents' workday. Parents responded enthusiastically to
the visits.

The Door—A Center of Alternatives, New York City,
provides comprehensive health, education, counseling, and
creative and physical arts services.The Door helps inner-city
young people become independent, self-sufficient adults through
a total-person approach.

Serving more than one thousand young people between the
ages of twelve and twenty each month, experienced professionals provide services free of charge.

The staff at The Door feel it is essential that the programs
take place in a setting which looks nothing like the schools or
bureaucratic facilities which have generated such strong
negative feelings among many young people.

The location is also distinguished by easy access from all
subway and bus lines—an important element in the program's
success in drawing young people. Michaele P. White, Administrator, Health Programs, described The Door's new (1988)
facility:

>   *Space at The Door is viewed as an essential element of*
> *our work with young people. In our new facility, open*
> *spaces, bright and cheerful colors, paintings, sculpture,*
> *and wall hangings (from our own creative and visual arts*
> *program) are used in non-traditional ways to encourage*
> *the free movement of young people from one program*
> *area to another. In this environment we can reduce the*
> *stress that can result when services are provided behind*

The Door. Katherine Criss Photography.

closed doors with labels reading "Substance Abuse Services," "Remedial Education Classes," or "Sexual Health Services."

Except for certain spaces such as the physical examination rooms where privacy is essential, every effort was made to minimize the use of high walls. We created functional spaces within an open, welcoming interior. This feeling of space and openness makes it easier for youth, who may be timid beneath their apparent bravado, to join in new activities—to venture into the health center, a counseling group, or remedial education class for the first time.

The Door program staff work hard to encourage young people to make wider and wider use of The Door's services and programs. The openness The Door communicates is the opposite of the locked doors, ruler-straight corridors, and bureaucratic rigidity young people so often encounter when seeking help. The openness young people find at The Door is an invitation to explore their talents and potential, White pointed out.

Church Settings

Many church facilities provide the multi-purpose space
needed by programs serving teens—classrooms, informal
meeting space, a large hall or gym, a kitchen, nursery, and a
playground. At first glance, the use of church facilities may
appear an ideal site for an adolescent pregnancy prevention or
care program. However, there are a number of issues to consider
before making the final decision to use a church location.

---

*The more positive publicity the program
gains for the local church,
the more supportive the host church may be.*

If the program is an activity sponsored by the church as a part
of the church's mission in meeting the needs of the community,
it may be fairly easy to gain initial support for the program. The
program will need to be constantly promoted with the church
staff and administrative committees to build a base of support
throughout the congregation. This support needs to remain
strong as committee membership and church leadership changes
from year to year.

Look for ways to publicize the program through the district,
regional, or national denominational newsletters or events. The
more positive publicity the program gains for the local church,
the more supportive the host church may be. Also, there may be
sources of funds at the regional or national level for special pilot
programs in local church settings. Find out if any exist, then go
after them.

If the arrangement with the church is not part of its program
goals, but is merely a rental agreement for use of the space, a
clear outline of needs is essential. Factors to be considered
include the actual space needs, the hours of program operation,
the population to be served, how potential expenses will be paid
(extra janitorial service needed, additional supplies, utilities,
etc.), and which church furnishings or equipment can be used for
the program (typewriters, copy machine, kitchen utensils).
Spelling this out at the beginning and setting times for the

review and evaluation of the program and rental agreement will go a long way toward avoiding problems once the program is underway.

---

*Try to anticipate problem areas
and address them before they arise.*

Whether or not the program concept is supported by the church congregation as a part of their mission, problems can arise when the program moves from the idea stage to implementation.

Suddenly, the congregation finds teenagers wandering in the hallways, unfamiliar cars filling the parking lot, extra janitorial service needed to keep the building clean, the responsibility for locking and unlocking the building being shared with non-church members, program and cleaning supplies being used at a rapid rate, and questions arising about insurance and liability issues. The same problems may occur, of course, in other community agencies.

However, the church has many more members and committees likely to be involved in decisions about facility use than do some other organizations. Leadership changes frequently. Issues over small, often routine matters, can become major sources of congregational concern.

It is also important to work closely with neighborhood people. Some business and residential neighborhoods will be concerned if the program brings an increased number of teens into their area, particularly if the teens are of a different ethnic or socio-economic background.

Try to overcome this early by meeting with neighborhood residents and/or businesses. Ask for their understanding, and assure them of your willingness to work with them if problems arise.

In a church setting, trying to anticipate problem areas and addressing them before they arise is important. Also, involving church members in the planning, resource development, and evaluation activities for the program will help increase their understanding of the program's goals and needs.

The Key—Creativity and Persistence

If a program is to be successful in attracting an adolescent
audience, the setting must provide a welcoming and comfortable
environment for that audience.

In selecting your program location, be creative and persistent.
Most successful adolescent pregnancy prevention and care
programs started small in a setting that was available and
affordable. The first program location may not have been an
ideal setting, but by keeping their vision of the ultimate goal, the
programs were able to expand and improve their locations and
settings over the years.

CHAPTER 8

Finding
The Funding

Ask an adolescent pregnancy program director to name the three things the program needs the most, and s/he may reply: 1) **money**, 2) **money** and 3) **money**. While an abundance of funding alone doesn't guarantee a well-run program that achieves its goals, adequate funding is critical to the program's ongoing operation, stability, and longevity.

To build a strong financial base, you need to look at your overall program in terms of the following:
- Vision
- Mission and purpose
- Goals and objectives
- Organizational management
- Fiscal accountability
- Evaluation process
- Marketing plan
- Advocacy role
- Long range plans

Each of these items plays a role in determining the funding sources your program can attract and how you'll go about it. Another way to think about this is to consider the linkage between four concepts:

Mission & Purpose

What your program is

$\downarrow$

Programs and Services
What you do

$\downarrow$

Program Participants
Whom you attract

$\downarrow$

Support (Financial & Other)
Where you get your support

TYPES OF FUNDING

Most programs need different types of funding at some point in their existence:

- Start up funding (seed money)
- Ongoing operational funding (annual budget)
- Long-term funding (expansion and future operation).

Funding sources for your program may be internal or external.

Internal sources are program generated and include:

- Program fees
- Organizational dues or memberships
- Sales of materials

External sources can be either monetary or in-kind and include:

- Private (foundations, corporations, individuals)
- Public (contributions, government grants, the United Way)
- Special events (labor intensive but may serve other goals such as publicity or volunteer involvement)
- Deferred (bequests, endowments)
- Annual campaign
- Capital campaign

Fundraising Takes Planning

Raising funds takes planning; it doesn't just happen. You must outline your financial needs, determine an appropriate fundraising process, define the roles and responsibilities for the staff and volunteers involved, identify potential funding sources, and develop a proposal or "case."

To develop a fundraising plan and the process for its implementation:

- **Define who benefits from your program,** what they're like, their needs, and reasons the community should be involved.
- **Identify all of the sources you might approach for funds**—in what amount and for what specific purpose.
- **Make sure your program looks like a good investment** for each potential funding source. For foundation requests, you may want to emphasize the positive program outcomes in human terms. For corporations, you'll want to focus on results, accomplishments, cost-effectiveness, and the benefits to the corporation.
- **Determine the protocol for your fundraising process.** Do your homework so you'll know the appropriate method for contacting each potential funding source.
- **Train your fundraising team, volunteers and staff, to feel comfortable asking for money.** Be positive—you're giving people an opportunity to invest in their community's future, and that should feel good. Skill in fundraising comes with experience, so practice—practice—practice.
- **Determine the appropriate spokesperson for your program** in contacting the various funding sources.

Remember, people give more readily to people they know, like, and trust.

- **Be persistent!** Never see failure as failure, but only an opportunity to improve your approach.

Local Sources of Funding

Successful local programs put together creative mixes of funding sources. In our current financial climate, successful programs look for a blending of public and private funding to build a secure financial base.

What types of funds are available in your community for programs serving youth? Is adolescent pregnancy prevention or care a priority with the United Way or other community-wide funding groups? Is dropout prevention a priority in your school district?

What types of related services are supported through local government funds—job training, nutrition, etc.? What private funds are available from local foundations, corporations, churches, or volunteer groups? What service clubs include in their annual activities fundraisers for local projects?

Local programs have received support from every group imaginable—from the local Sheriff's Department to the Garden Club. Don't overlook any potential funding source.

Marilyn Steele, Program Officer for the Charles Stewart Mott Foundation, suggests that seeking funding close to home is the best source for many local prevention and care programs. Since public tax moneys comprise a large part of the human service program funding in our country, she stressed the need for local community program providers to know the types of funds available at state and local government levels.

Most education, health care, and social service funding starts at the state level and funnels down to the county and city level. Thus, local program providers must become very familiar not only with the funding sources, but also with the funding priorities that have been established by state and local funding sources.

In addition to government funding, a variety of other local funding sources should be explored:

- **Community Foundations.** Look at their annual reports to determine the funding priorities, operating practices, timelines, and previous grant recipients.
- **Corporations.** Many contribute funds through public affairs departments, marketing departments, a local corporate foundation, or through the foundation associated with their national headquarters.
- **Trust Departments.** Local banks have trust officers who look for places to donate funds from the trusts they are managing. Ask a bank trust officer to serve on your Advisory Board.
- **Service Clubs/Auxiliaries.** These groups often look for projects or programs to support through their annual fundraising events.
- **Churches and Synagogues.** These provide multiple sources for funding, program support, and volunteers. Most have groups that look for special projects. Large denominations have funds designated for social causes, particularly for new efforts by local congregations.
- **Individuals.** The largest source of charitable funding given in our country each year comes from individuals. Don't overlook this important funding source. There are people in your hometown who give money. Your role is to give them an opportunity to give it to your program.

Even if you have very little money, you can start small projects. The success of those small projects may be the foundation on which to raise more funding. Barbara Ziegler, chairperson, Mecklenburg Council on Adolescent Pregnancy (MCAP), said, "It's important to know you don't have to get $5000 before you can do anything. You can do a lot with $500—posters, TeenHelp cards, service directory. We've produced manuals on how to do clergy conferences and how to do a health fair, each at little cost. You could do a junior high health fair with almost no money."

Working with Advisory Board

Funding efforts can be helped dramatically with the aid of an active community-wide advisory board. Recently in Boulder,

Colorado, a board member from IBM requested corporate community service funds to develop a toddler outdoor play yard for the **Teen Parenting Program** in the **Boulder Valley School District.** IBM granted $1,000 for this project. Kiwanis donated about $1,500, and Kiwanis members put up the fence around the play yard.

Gloria Parmerlee-Greiner, Director, commented:

> *To get these things to happen, I use our Advisory Board. When we need something, we call and ask. We also use the school newspaper, the Council of Churches, Chamber of Commerce, the Lions Club. When I hear of a new organization, I phone immediately to explain our program and our needs.*
>
> *I've served on several other boards, too. For this kind of networking, you have to be available to help them, too. You have to be ready to speak to their groups at almost any time.*

Involving Clients and Volunteers

Judy Peterson directs **Birth, Education, Training and Acceptance Program (BETA), Orlando, Florida,** a private organization providing, in cooperation with the local school district, social, health, and educational services to young mothers and their children.

BETA doesn't accept government funding. Its $350,000 annual budget comes from corporate and private donations. Peterson explained:

> *Theoretically we can't get $350,000 without govern-ment funds, but neither can we fail. Where would these girls go? You open your doors every day.*
>
> *The first money I got was because I got on the phone and called people—people from cocktail parties, for instance, who had said, "Can I do something?"*
>
> *I called and said, "We have a mortgage payment of $400/month, I need utilities, and this is my monthly budget. How much can you give? Five dollars? Twenty*

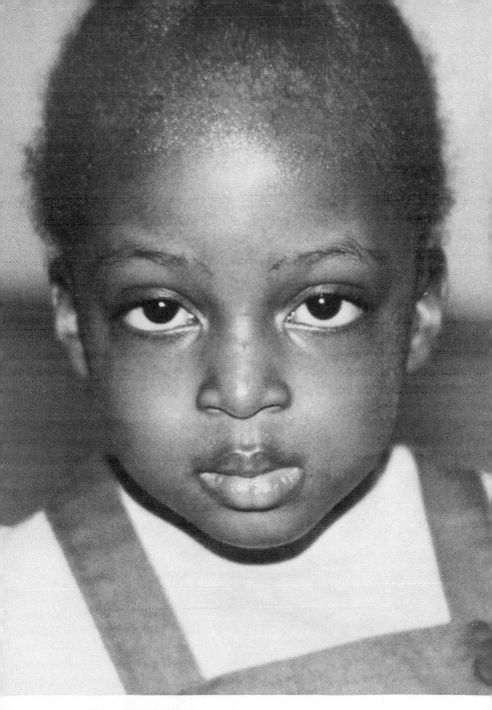

BETA client, Orlando, Florida

*dollars a month?" Nearly everyone gave something. And
people have always volunteered. We depend a great deal
on volunteers.*

*Our clients are great fundraisers. They go back into the
community and tell our story. When people hear what
we're doing, they want to help.*

*I excel in persistence. The $350,000 comes mostly from
individuals, churches, and civic groups plus about ten
percent from private philanthropic grants. People are
frustrated with being bombarded all day long with
problems they can't solve.*

*BETA gives them an opportunity to do something
direct. They know exactly where their money is going, they
know exactly what it does, and they know exactly the
problem they're helping to solve. That takes care of some
of their frustration. They know they're providing nurturing
care for a very young baby, putting a roof over their
heads, tangible things.*

Each year BETA raises nearly $20,000 through about a
thousand volunteers wrapping Christmas gifts for one day in two
malls for a fee.

"Our volunteers are one of our biggest PR and fundraising
tools," Peterson commented. "Their hearts are with BETA, and
they know what we're doing."

Funding for Rural Programs

David Reese, Director, **Southwest District Health Department, Caldwell, Idaho,** said the key issue for rural programs
seeking funding is the numbers game.

Often, programs from small communities are competing with
urban programs where the numbers of people needing to be
served are immense. To compete, he suggests that rural programs try to regionalize a project in order to serve a larger
geographic area.

Rural areas have significant social problems including
poverty, isolation, a shortage of resources, and traditions of
apathy and neglect. Outreach to potential program participants is

difficult when long distances are involved. Travel to a program
site may not be possible for some people, especially children
and adolescents.

Reese said program directors need to be realistic about costs
for implementing a program in a rural area. They need to build
into any program funding proposal accurate expense figures for
travel, mileage, postage, and other costs that may be higher for a
rural program. According to Reese:

> *In rural areas, we're isolated, and that can inhibit*
> *effective fundraising. We can't attend a lot of meetings to*
> *meet key people. We have a shortage of people with*
> *fundraising and grant writing expertise.*
>
> *To overcome these barriers, people in rural areas need*
> *to get involved in national or regional organizations. We*
> *need to contact foundation or government agency people*
> *when we're traveling to other meetings. We need to talk*
> *with the appropriate people in the federal office in our*
> *region to learn what resources are available and what*
> *requests for proposals will be announced. Our networking*
> *efforts have to be a constant priority to cultivate potential*
> *funding sources.*
>
> *Sometimes a program can attract the attention of a*
> *funder because of its rurality. The program may be*
> *located in an area that a particular funder wants to serve.*
> *Rural program directors need to point out honestly the*
> *shortage of resources to potential funding sources. By*
> *funding your program, the funder could provide technical*
> *assistance that would empower you to help increase the*
> *skills of other program providers in your area.*

Other ways to overcome fundraising barriers in rural areas,
according to Reese, include finding an organization within the
community to use as the base for developing a program. Some
rural areas may not have youth agencies or even a hospital. They
will have a school, a health delivery system of some kind, and
an Extension Service contact for the county who is linked to the
land-grant college in the state.

These programs will have the capacity to administer a program. Within these existing organizations, you may find someone who will be willing to give your program a mailing address, computer time, or access to other needed program resources.

Reese believes program providers in rural areas need to be realistic about the time frame for developing major program funding. The first catch is the hardest. It may take from three to ten years for the "big hit."

Public Funding

Federal, state and local government funding sources play a critical role in adolescent pregnancy program funding. The federal budget sets overall spending priorities for the federal government which determines, in many cases, the amount of funds available to state and local community programs.

When looking at public funding sources for your adolescent pregnancy program, check with city or county departments that relate to youth programming and funding. What funds do they receive through the state?

What funds might be locally generated? What sources provide program funds for maternal/child health, vocational education, youth employment, child nutrition, juvenile justice, child welfare, adoption assistance, family planning, child abuse and neglect, housing, or other education, health or social service programs that impact young people?

Talk with people in your community who know the system, know where the funds are, and know what they might be used for in terms of programming. Local elected officials are a good place to start.

Members of the school board, city council, county board of supervisors, and city or county commissions should be good resources to identify possible public funding sources. Staff members of local government agencies who deal with the funding of local programs and services will also provide valuable information.

Federal government agencies have regional offices through-out the country. Check with the following regional offices in

your area to learn about programs, training, or funding which
might be of assistance for your program:

- **Department of Labor**—Includes the Job Training Partnership Act (JTPA) that provides training and employment
  services, as well as the federal Youth: 2000 initiative
  focused on education, training, and support services
  for youth.
- **Department of Health and Human Services:** Includes
  numerous programs in DHHS relating to teen pregnancy
  prevention, including the Office of Adolescent Pregnancy
  Programs (OAPP) which funds adolescent pregnancy prevention and care programs, National Center for Child
  Abuse and Neglect (NCCAN), Maternal and Child Health
  (MCH), and the Office of Human Development Services
  (OHDS), which supervises Head Start, child abuse, foster
  care adoption assistance, and child welfare services.
  Department of Education: Includes some vocational and
  special education funds; many programs related to adoles-
  cent pregnancy in the past have been scaled back or
  eliminated.
- **Department of Justice:** Includes the Office of Juvenile
  Justice and Delinquency Prevention (OJJDP).
- **ACTION:** Includes the VISTA program which provides
  workers who could assist in local community resource
  development.
- **Department of Defense:** Includes family advocacy
  programs for military families and a "Personal Excellence
  Initiative" as part of **Youth: 2000.**

At the state level, some agencies are beginning to provide
innovative funding for local adolescent pregnancy and parenting
programs.

The State Department of Health in Oklahoma targeted special
funding to underwrite planning grants for adolescent pregnancy
programs in local communities. The funding grants were
awarded to collaborative community proposals to develop a
broad-based community task force, implement a teen pregnancy
prevention needs assessment in the local community, and outline
a detailed community plan for addressing the identified needs.

Marilyn Lanphier, Director of **Adolescent Health Services**
for the **Oklahoma Department of Health,** said:

>   *More and more, state agencies are recognizing the
>   need to assist local communities in identifying their own
>   program priorities related to adolescent pregnancy pre-
>   vention. Local programs have the potential for being more
>   effective over time if there is ownership by the local
>   community in the service being delivered.*
>
>   *As public funding becomes more limited in many states
>   due to federal budget cuts and local economic factors, it is
>   the responsibility of the state agencies to help local
>   communities ensure that needed health care and related
>   services are delivered.*
>
>   *This is especially true for adolescent pregnancy
>   programs. We can't let budget cuts keep our local pro-
>   grams from focusing on prevention activities for our kids.
>   Supporting collaborative, well-planned community
>   programs will save the state a great deal of money in the
>   long term.*

Always remember that state government agencies receiving federal funds have been mandated to have formal linkages with community agencies and organizations. They need
you, too!

Corporate Funding

Corporations often budget money for community service.
Once you've determined a business or corporation to contact,
find out how they fund an organization or program. Is there an
application form or deadline? Do they have meetings at set times
of the year to consider proposals? Does the corporation have a
separate foundation? What are the various sources of support
within the corporation?

  • Look for companies close to home. Is there a branch office
    or a plant of a major company located in your community?
    Check with the Chamber of Commerce to get a listing of
    the companies with information on what they do and how

many people they employ. What local consumer-oriented businesses in your area either employ young people or target the youth market for their products or services?

- Get to know people in, or with connections to, the corporations. If possible, meet with the person who has responsibility for allocating funds.
- Link your program to the corporation's goals or the improvement of the community's quality of life whenever possible. For example, helping teens complete their education, gain job skills, and build stable families should decrease school dropout, unemployment, welfare dependency, and other less desirable conditions while contributing to the number and preparation of the skilled labor force in the area.
- Find ways to let people within the corporation know what your program is doing. Add them to your mailing list, recruit volunteers from the corporation for your program, put your clients' success stories in their corporate newsletters, have a program display in their employee dining area. Be creative!
- Secure letters of support from people who have credibility with the leadership in the company.
- Identify in-kind services which they could provide, such as legal or accounting support, personnel or financial development assistance, securing equipment or furniture, volunteer time, etc.
- Once you have received funding, give appropriate recognition and visibility to the sponsoring organization. Continue to expand and nurture the relationship as a base for future funding.

Foundation Funding

For foundation funding, contact the foundation's office to secure a copy of their recent annual report and information about the foundation's funding priorities and application process.

Dr. Steele of the **Mott Foundation** says, "Large national or regional foundations have a special role to play in developing and testing adolescent pregnancy prevention and care

interventions. They often provide the funding for major projects
of national scope to:

- Identify the problem
- Develop intervention strategies
- Test a pilot project
- Disseminate results
- Replicate the effective intervention

"Or, very simply, their role is to **investigate, demonstrate,
test, disseminate, and replicate.** New, local programs will
seldom be of this scale, and they need to look for community or
area foundations more likely to fund their activities.

"The biggest mistake local programs make when seeking
foundation funding is failing to do their homework. Unless a
proposal fits a particular foundation's interests and restrictions,
the local program is wasting time and postage in applying," Dr.
Steele stressed.

Yusef Mgeni, former Program Officer for the **Northwest
Area Foundation**, echoes that comment when he suggests that
program providers "hunt where the ducks are." In other words,
look for the foundations whose priorities and guidelines closely
match the mission and goals of your program.

Mgeni, too, stresses that doing your homework is time well
spent. Check the funding directories in your local library to learn
which foundations give to your kind of program, in what area,
and in what amounts.

Contact previous grantees to find out how a specific foundation prefers to be approached.

Once you have determined foundations appropriate to
contact, call and talk with a program officer. If they indicate
they might have some interest in your program, send them a
formal letter of inquiry (three pages maximum) describing:

- who you are
- what you want
- the amount requested
- the difference your program will make.

In the letter, ask if the foundation would like to receive a full
proposal. They will let you know. Send proposals only to
funders expressing an interest in the project.

Mgeni cautions program providers not to duplicate fifty copies of the identical proposal and mail them to every foundation address possible. Again, you are wasting your time and their time. According to Mgeni, the Northwest Area Foundation funds about ninety percent of the proposals they solicit and rejects about ninety-eight per cent of the unsolicited proposals they receive.

Proposal Writing Hints

Numerous guides on writing proposals are available in local libraries, and every state has as least one major funding library. Each source may outline the major parts of a proposal in a little different manner, but most include these general categories:
- Cover letter
- Table of contents
- Statement of need/ definition of problem
- Project description—what you're going to do and the anticipated outcomes
- Staff and organizational capability
- Budget—project and organizational
- Evaluation method
- Plan for future funding
- History of the organization
- Support materials: List of board of directors, resumes of project staff, IRS letter of tax-exempt status, selected organizational descriptive materials, and letters of support from key community groups indicating their interest in working with your program (e.g., school administrators, health professionals, youth agencies, the city or county government).

Common Mistakes in Proposal Writing
- **Failing to do your homework.** Research potential grant-makers thoroughly. What do they fund? In what amount? When?
- **Not following the application directions.** Whether a foundation or government grant, most groups offering the grants will outline the information they wish to receive

from applicants and indicate their time frame. Follow their outline. If you're unclear about something, call them.

- **Project doesn't fit the priorities or focus of the funding source . . . or, the "great contortions act."** This is a trap into which programs can easily fall. We need funding. Funding is available, though it really doesn't fit our main mission and goals. But we come up with a way (through great mental and programmatic contortions) and a rationale for applying. Unfortunately, this may serve to cloud your program's focus and steer it off course on the achievement of its program goals.
- **Shotgun proposals.** A reminder again to tailor proposals to the specific priorities, application procedures, and focus of the individual funding sources. It may seem less time consuming to duplicate several dozen identical proposals and mail them to multiple funding sources, but your chances of being selected with that approach are probably slim to none.
- **Too long and confused.** We've all read really good proposals and really bad proposals, and the difference was apparent. Often, program providers feel more is better when it comes to writing a proposal, but that's not so. When you write more than five pages for the body of a corporate proposal or ten pages for a foundation proposal, you probably need to edit. Make sure the text of the proposal clearly and simply outlines what you're going to do, how you're going to do it, and how you'll know if it's been successful.
- **Fuzzy language.** Make your writing clear, concise, and easy to read. This is no time to impress someone with the word of the day on your desk calendar. Avoid using acronyms, terms, or phrases that may be common to your organization but not to funders who know nothing about your program. Use positive action terms and future oriented language—it's much more appealing.
- **Twisted statistics.** Use all data as accurately as possible. Use firm numbers, not subjective or undocumented data as facts.

- **Promising more than you can deliver.** This happens to a lot of programs. Don't overstate the case in terms of what can be delivered or what your program will do. This can be a set-up for failure.
- **Inattention to details.** Usually as a result of a tight deadline, little things like page numbers get omitted, or typing errors don't get corrected. Proof the proposal yourself, and have an objective third party look it over to make sure it's clear and reads well.

Special Events

Special events can't be relied upon magically to produce your program's annual operating budget through one day's event, but their payoffs may involve more than fundraising. The community visibility, participant involvement, new contributor prospects, and media coverage that special events offer can help keep your program in the public's eye.

The challenge in developing a special event is to find the right one for your program.

The **Sisterhood of Black Single Mothers, Brooklyn, New York,** uses a number of special events not only to raise funds, but to offer opportunities for building community awarenss and involvement. One event is the annual "Positive Fatherhood Awards Ceremony" where local men are recognized for their exemplary participation with their families and communities. Food, entertainment, and inspirational speakers are included in the festivities. A souvenir journal is prepared to commemorate the event through the sale of ads to local businesses. Tickets to attend the event are also sold.

The possibilities for special events are endless. Once the right event is determined, dedicated volunteers, at least a minimal budget for expenses and promotion, ample planning time, and good organization are essential. Special events are hard work and labor intensive, even when they fail. Creativity, timing, and even the weather can make the difference between success and failure.

The booklet, "Discover Total Resources: A Guide for Nonprofits," prepared by the Mellon Bank Corporation, shares the following suggestions for planning a special event:

- Allow plenty of lead time for planning and developing community support. Too many great ideas fail due to poor timing and organization.
- Be creative. Choose an event that relates to your good work.
- Develop a budget and planning schedule—then stick to them. Keep detailed records for future planning, if it's to become an annual event.
- Recruit volunteers to form a central planning committee. Have them recruit others to serve as workers. Use your teens!
- Consider selling advertising space in a program and/or promotional materials. In this way, local businesses can be spotlighted.
- Talk to people who have organized successful fundraising events in your area. Ask them how they did it.

An excellent source for local program fundraising ideas and strategies is *The Grassroots Fundraising Book* (1982: Contemporary Books, Inc.), by Joan Flanagan. This book has been a classic for grassroots fundraising activities for many years.

Long-term Funding and Resources

Successful programs need multiple anchors, meaning different sources for funding and resources. A program that has all funds coming from one or two short-term grants faces a serious risk of significant cutbacks when those grants end. Often, foundations, corporations, or government agencies fund innovative pilot or demonstration projects, but are not interested in providing long-term support once a program is operational.

Most programs have developed a piecemeal approach to the securing of funds and resources, using a mix of governmental, charitable, volunteer, and in-kind support, whatever is available. This approach takes considerable energy and ingenuity, as the various funding sources often have vastly differing limitations, reporting requirements, and fiscal years.

After a few years, many independent programs seek to become institutionalized either by associating with a health, educational, or social service agency, or by affiliating with an umbrella funding source such as the community United Way. A major benefit of becoming institutionalized is to secure stable, long-term funding. This can be a strenuous process loaded with potential delays and political maneuverings, but is usually worth the effort.

If your program has not established non-profit, tax-exempt, 501(c)(3) IRS status, you may wish to consider doing so to expand your long-term funding options. Programs already associated with an institution that is prohibited from special fundraising, such as a school system, may wish to establish a separate non-profit corporation to expand their financial support opportunities. See Chapter Five.

Coping with Cutbacks

Cutbacks are a reality with any adolescent pregnancy prevention or care program receiving public or even private funding at present. Cutbacks imply change—unwanted change. Cutbacks are painful, can compromise important services to teens, and occasionally can be fatal to the entire program.

In the development of your long-range strategic plan, you should include contingency plans in the event that cuts occur. Thinking through your options ahead of time will help your program avoid crisis management and, hopefully, reduce long-term damage to the services delivered to teens. If your program relies heavily on a network of services involving other agencies, all of you should develop a plan to cope in the event that cutbacks occur to any of the participating agencies.

If cutbacks occur, it is critical that program directors provide information for the staff and the participants in a timely and accurate manner. There is a tremendous need for a sense of security during a period of cutbacks in a program. Without clear and constant communication, the rumor mill can run rampant, damaging staff morale and impacting negatively upon the delivery of services to the teen participants.

Adolescent pregnancy care programs, in particular, can be stressful to administer, given the crisis situations with which the programs must deal. Adding internal stress from uncertainty

created by poorly planned or managed cutbacks can be
devastating.

Responding to a NOAPP questionnaire which asked, "How
have you handled funding cuts?" program directors echoed,
"Poorly," "With agony," "Maintained the strain," "A constant
problem," and similar themes. Most indicated they initially cut
staff, reduced services, or decreased support services such as
outreach or transportation.

One program director said, "We cut back on supplies. So far,
we have always recovered and found replacement sources of
income. In the interim, we bite the bullet which is stressful. We
try to give lots of peer support."

As to how they plan to handle future cuts, many of the
program directors said they will "brainstorm, improvise, and
overcome!"

Selling Program to School District

Sherry Betts, Director of Services for **Adolescent Family
Education, Tucson, Arizona,** devised successful strategies for
coping with funding cutbacks.

Betts and Anne Martinez, Nurse, were first hired under a
grant to help expand services of a small academic program for
pregnant and parenting teens. Both are still with the program
which has grown large (250 clients enrolled per year) and
comprehensive. Growth occurred for several reasons.

The original grant funding was for prenatal health education,
outreach, follow-up and counseling. Betts and Martinez started
networking with community services. They continued to write
grants, but with each one, managed to have the school district
pick up part of the funding annually.

Betts explained, "During the years we relied on grants, we
did a thorough evaluation of the impact of the services the grant
funded. As the grant money diminished, we were able to show
the value of the service and justify the district picking up that
funding."

A few years ago the program had to move, and the district
had little money or space for them. Betts described the efforts
that changed that scenario:

*We did a great deal of work in the community. We
worked with the school board, and we had parents talk
with the central administrators and with board members.
Parents attended school board meetings and talked about
their children, what this program meant to them, and
where their children would be without it. We built knowledge and support, and at a time the district was strapped
for money, they put nearly three million dollars into a
building for us.*

*Programs like ours tend to go off and do their own
thing until they're threatened. This was a good opportunity for us, and we're enjoying a great deal of support
from the district.*

One year Betts was threatened with a major budget cut. She
reacted by going to the school district's Finance Department to
learn how Average Daily Attendance (ADA—the major source
of school funding) was figured. She multiplied the dollar amount
the district received for each student by the number of retrieved
dropouts in her program, students who wouldn't be in school if
there were no Adolescent Family Education services. Then she
figured actual program costs in terms of salaries, supplies,
utilities, and space, then compared that with the state aid.

"I discovered that counting only retrieved drops, we were
bringing in at least $50,000 above the program's costs. I pre-
sented that to the central administrators, and our budget was
restored in full," she reported.

Betts cautioned that the method of figuring the amount of
funding per pupil may vary from state to state, and that the
formula tends to be quite complicated due to special funding for
various services offered within the schools.

You Can Do It

Fundraising is an essential part of any program's operation.
In most cases, fundraising skills are acquired skills. It takes
resourcefulness, marketing your program in positive terms, and
knowing what you need. It involves training staff and volunteers
to assist with fundraising efforts, being assertive about

requesting funding from a variety of sources, and asking for advice or in-kind assistance when you can't get dollars. It requires helping others see the value of supporting your program. Not losing sight of your vision is integral to fundraising.

Good fundraising means showing that your program is cost-effective, that it is making a difference, and that, by serving young people, it is future-oriented. Good fundraising involves showing the benefits for the participants and the benefits for the funder.

Successful fundraising takes time, planning, and finding the right people to contact the right sources with the right program ideas. In all communities, there are people who know how to raise money, there are people who would like to learn how to raise money, and there are potential sources of funding for your program.

Funding sources are going to give their money to some program . . . your job is to convince them that yours is the program to fund.

CHAPTER **9**

Evaluating
Your Effectiveness

Evaluation is a critical but often overlooked function of adolescent pregnancy prevention and care programs. Good evaluation takes thought, careful planning, and adequate funding to be effective. Whether a multi-site, comprehensive program in a large urban area or a small, single room program in a rural area, an appropriate evaluation method can be designed and implemented.

What Is Evaluation?

Basically, program evaluation is the systematic collection, analysis, and interpretation of information. Effective evaluation assists in program planning and decision-making. It indicates which efforts are the most successful, and enables you to allocate resources to the areas that have documented the greatest achievement of the desired program results.

Evaluation helps a program stay on track by providing an objective method for monitoring the client's needs, program

processes, and program outcomes on an on-going basis. It helps
you make mid-course corrections, broaden your support in the
larger community, and plan for the future.

Evaluation is used to ensure that the services being provided
are responsive to client, organization, and community needs. It
is concerned with the types of interventions used, by whom,
toward what ends, under what conditions, for whom, at what
costs, and with what benefits.

Why Evaluation Is Important

Who cares about evaluation data other than researchers and
statisticians? Both funders and program providers are becoming
more and more sophisticated today in terms of evaluation.
Funders want to know if their monetary investment is generating
a positive return. They want to know if their funding is making a
difference. And they certainly have a right to know what's
happening in a program they're underwriting.

Likewise, program providers want to know if the work
they're doing is having an impact. Are they moving toward the
achievement of the goals established for the program? If not,
they may be wasting valuable time and resources that could be
better spent approaching the problem in another way.

Georgia Chaffee, principal, **Teenage Parent Program,
Louisville, Kentucky,** commented:

> *When you can show in numbers that you're successful,
> when you have parents saying, "My child's attitude has
> changed. She's interested in school. She's responsible,"
> and you have kids saying the program has changed their
> lives, you can take those comments and use them for fund-
> ing. We have tremendous support from the state, and I
> think that comes from clearly describing the successes we
> have.*
>
> *You have to show you're keeping kids in school and
> they're earning diplomas. You try to be friends with
> people next to the governor, and put the right kind of
> people on your advisory council. But in addition to all
> this, the funding depends on documenting your successes.*

Uses of Evaluation Information

Julia Littell, former coordinator of research and evaluation for the Family Resource Coalition's newsletter, *FRC Report,* outlined the uses of evaluation in a newsletter article as follows:

- **Describing the service delivery system.** What is the program doing? Why? How? Descriptions of program processes and rationales enable providers to understand service delivery activities and to describe them to outsiders.
- **Documentation.** How much of what services are provided? For whom? When? Where? At what costs? This data can be gathered from simple record-keeping systems. It helps others to understand what the program is doing and how it works.
- **Program planning and development.** What services, changes, or improvements are needed? Sound programs are based on regular feedback about the client's needs, the service delivery procedures, and the outcomes. This information can be used to create or modify services in response to changing individual, organization, or community needs.
- **Assessing program outcomes.** What is the program's impact on its clients and the community? What results have been achieved? Sound outcome evaluations are complex and require expertise in the development of the evaluation instruments and assessment.
- **Contributing to knowledge in the field.** Adolescent pregnancy programs usually don't lend themselves to significant short-term results. Prevention programs, especially, require longitudinal studies to evaluate accurately the impact of a particular intervention. Sophisticated studies are needed to test the effectiveness of various service delivery models, and to determine which of them are most effective for specific target populations.
- **Developing program models for replication.** Careful documentation of a program's experiences, its implementation processes, the problems encountered, solutions attempted, and expected or achieved results can be made available for others to use.

- **Developing evaluation instruments and methods.** What evaluation techniques and instruments work well in specific settings? For different populations? By sharing reliable instruments and useful techniques, others can be saved the time and trouble of reinventing the wheel.

When to Start

Ideally, the evaluation process should be planned from the beginning as a part of the development of the total program proposal. However, for many programs, this doesn't happen. Even as a program is being planned, there is usually too much to do with too few staff and limited resources to focus significant attention on the planning and implementation of an evaluation process.

Coupled with the concerns of limited staff, time, and resources may be a lack of understanding of how to design and implement an appropriate evaluation process and the importance of doing so from the beginning. Program evaluation may shift to the back burner partly due to the mystique surrounding the evaluation activity which conjures up images of time-consuming analysis and paperwork.

Some program providers may be more comfortable discussing their program using personal success stories rather than documenting their success in terms of numerical data. Certainly, vignettes and testimonies of participants touch the emotions of the audience and have a place in marketing your program to your supporters. Emotional responses may lose their impact, however, when funding sources take pencil to paper and determine the program cost per participant.

Ann Sandven, Project Director of **CONNECT, Nampa, Idaho,** commented:

> *My least favorite activity is data collection—but I do a lot of it. We do it because we're a research project and we have to, but I think more and more the emphasis is for programs to show they work. If you can't prove they work, it's hard to go to foundations and ask for more money.*

*We have an intake form and an outcome form that's
filled out within a month of our clients' giving birth. We
also have a client-infant status form where we look at
mother and baby. How are they doing at six months,
twelve months, eighteen and twenty-four months?*

*It's important to plan an evaluation component from
the very beginning. Think about your objectives, how
you'll measure them. Even though there will be change,
build the evaluation in right at the start because it's
almost impossible to go back and recreate that
information.*

David Reese, who developed the **CONNECT** program,
concurred in the importance of including evaluation in the
initial program proposal. "Make sure the real costs of the
evaluation process are built into the program budget, including staff time, resources, and outside research assistance,"
he suggested. "It's important to involve an expert as early in
the process as you possibly can. Waiting until the program is
underway makes it more difficult to implement an effective
evaluation process because you can't go back and gather
needed data. It's hard to put on your evaluation shoes after
you've started running," Reese pointed out.

Where to Start

Fern Marx, Project Director with the Wellesley College
Center for Research on Women, says, "Program providers
understand the need for and the basic uses of evaluation. Unfortunately, they're not always sure where or how to start, and too
often get lost in the process."

Where is a starting point? Where do program staff members
find people with the knowledge and skills to help them decide
the type of evaluation they need?

According to researcher Dennis McBride, you can start by
"just asking around." How are other programs in your community evaluating their activities? What kind of evaluation models
and instruments are they using? How did they develop their
evaluation process? Who helped them?

Contact program planning groups such as the United Way to learn the type of technical assistance they might provide in the area of evaluation. Universities might be helpful, depending upon their experience with your type of program and their understanding of agencies and non-profit operations. If you're making cold calls to a university to ask about possible technical assistance, contact the social work or sociology department.

Two good resources from the Data Archive on Adolescent Pregnancy and Pregnancy Prevention (DAAPPP) are *Evaluating and Monitoring Programs for Pregnant and Parenting Teens* and *Sourcebook of Comparison Data for Evaluating Adolescent Pregnancy and Parenting Programs.* (See Bibliography.)

Types of Program Evaluations

According to researcher Susan Philliber, there are four types of evaluations associated with adolescent pregnancy programs:
1) **Needs assessments.** What do we need to do?
2) **Process evaluations.** Is the program being carried out as planned? Are we doing what the program said it would do?
3) **Impact evaluations.** What are the program's results? How does the status of the situation compare before and after the program implementation?
4) **Cost effectiveness evaluations.** What did it cost? Compare the resource investment with the program results.

Process evaluations may be the easiest and most appropriate types of evaluation for many programs. According to Fern Marx, a good process evaluation can be as simple as setting up a checklist logging what your program did and how. The process evaluation involves keeping the following information:
• **What was done—the actual implementation process?**
• **How was it done—using what methods?.**

If clear goals and success criteria are defined at the beginning, according to Marx, the process evaluation will allow program staff to say, "Yes, we did what we planned to do."

Goals and Objectives

Whether a prevention or care program, all program evaluation models must start with clear program goals and objectives.

Without those, you have no idea what you're doing or what you need to be measuring.

Various descriptions are used to differentiate the words *goals* and *objectives*. Basically, a goal is a general task to be achieved. Goals relate to the overall mission of the program and describe a desired future program status. A goal may, and most often does, have multiple objectives necessary to its achievement.

For example, a goal for an adolescent pregnancy prevention program in a youth group setting might be: "To provide an adolescent pregnancy prevention educational program for all students in sixth grade during the school year."

Objectives fall under the goal and are more specific and measurable. They may be actions that will be done, items that will be produced, or changes that will be accomplished to achieve the overall goal.

According to Philliber, adolescent pregnancy program objectives may fall into four different categories:

1) **Process objectives.** Things the staff will do or provide in carrying out the program: "To provide a two-hour weekly adolescent pregnancy prevention after-school program for sixth and seventh grade participants in the Community Youth Program for thirty-six weeks during the 1989-1990 school year."

2) **Program objectives.** Tangible products that will be produced: "To produce a thirty-six-lesson activity work-book to use with participants in the after-school Community Youth Program adolescent pregnancy prevention program."

3) **Outcome objectives.** What the clients or participants will do in the short-term as a result of the program: "To increase knowledge of participants in the adolescent pregnancy prevention after-school program in terms of . . ."

4. **Impact objectives.** Long-range changes among clients or a larger target population expected as a result of the program: "To reduce the number of adolescent pregnancies during their intermediate and high school years by ten percent among the participants in the adolescent pregnancy prevention program."

To carry out the goals and objectives, program providers will need to outline the specific action steps that must occur. This activity adds more detailed information and describes exactly *who* will do *what* by *when* to get things done and *what* resources are required to make it all happen.

Developing Your Evaluation Model

McBride emphasized that coming up with one single best model is difficult since agencies have personalities of their own. At the least, most programs should be able to provide a fairly thorough process evaluation to see if the program implementation is actually being carried out as planned.

A beginning step, McBride said, is to agree on the success criteria. Some program evaluation plans get lost at the outset if no clear criteria is identified as the measure determining if the program is carrying out its purpose and achieving its goals. Without clearly outlined criteria as a standard, you'll have no way of knowing when you've achieved success in meeting your goals.

The evaluation should tell you if you are implementing your process as planned, and should be integrated into the daily program activities.

Begin slowly, and build on your initial evaluation effort. Set yourself up to succeed, rather than falling into failure by over-extending yourself at the beginning. The process can be simple enough to put on a personal computer and the results used to prepare reports.

In choosing an evaluation strategy for your program, you'll want to start by asking some basic questions:

1) **What are the program's purposes for the evaluation?**
2) **What types of information are needed?**
3) **How will it be used?**
4) **What resources are available to plan and carry out the evaluation?** (Funding, staff time, expertise.)

The evaluation, he cautioned, can't lead the project. The evaluation should be designed to test accurately the intervention that is there. The program design can't be changed just to make the evaluation look good.

Basic Steps to Consider

Lynn E. Pooley and Littell, in their *Family Resource Program Builder* (1986: Family Resource Coalition), identified some basic steps for setting up a program evaluation process:

1) **Identify and secure input from key groups.** Determine who will use or be interested in the results, and involve them as part of the evaluation team—staff, administrators, board of directors, funders.

2) **Review and refine program goals and objectives.** Measurable goals and objectives are essential for good evaluation and program planning. They bring the program's mission down to a level where service delivery and evaluation tasks are clear.

3) **Identify purpose(s) of your evaluation.** This is important to do before the detailed design is planned. What are the purposes of the evaluation, and how will the data be used?

4) **Define roles and responsibilities.** Who will do what in carrying out the evaluation? Good evaluation is often the result of a team effort. It is wise, however, to select one person who will have the overall responsibility for coordinating the project.

5) **Identify your evaluation questions.** Good evaluation questions are those that can be answered by data that a program has or can obtain, and will provide useful answers for program decision making.

6) **Design your evaluation tool.** The evaluation tool needs to flow logically from the questions to be answered, the current needs for information, and the program's stated objectives. The overall program design should be comprised of the following:

    a. What information is needed, and how will it be measured?

    b. Who can best provide this information? Define who will be included in the evaluation and how those people will be selected. You may want to gather data from several different sources—participants, direct service personnel, and program administrator.

    c. How and when will the data be collected? The data collection can include multiple methods. You will want to

collect data that determines the participants' characteristics
and needs, a resource analysis of the financial, human, and
material assets being used, basic service statistics, and the
degree of client satisfaction.

**d. How will the quality of information be assessed in
terms of validity and reliability?** The validity refers to
the instrument used measuring what it says it measures.
Reliability should show it measures consistently.

7. **Develop an evaluation plan.** Think through a clear plan
   before collecting data. Otherwise, you may collect, then
   wonder what to do with it and how to make sense of it.

8. **Pilot test the evaluation plan.** Try out the evaluation
   instruments and procedures, looking for problem areas.
   Are the instructions and format clear? Does the staff
   understand the process?

9. **Implement your plan.** Revise the plan as needed following the pilot test, and then begin the full implementation of
   your plan.

10. **Summarize, analyze, and interpret your data.** There are
    different ways to organize data. Decide the best way to
    present an accurate assessment of your information. This
    should be an ongoing process that will assist in monitoring
    the program.

11. **Disseminate the findings.** Determine an appropriate way
    to share the data with co-workers, board members,
    program participants, and other key groups.

12. **Incorporate your findings into your program planning
    process.** Evaluation data should be one of many factors
    considered as you plan for the future of your program.

Involve Staff and Others

Program staff need to be involved in each step of the evaluation design. Sometimes staff in adolescent pregnancy programs
are overloaded in the daily program operation, and view the
collection of data as an unnecessary, time-consuming activity.
When staff understand the reasons certain data is to be collected
and how that data will be used, they're less likely to resist
participating in the evaluation process. It's essential that the

evaluation process be presented in a positive manner that helps staff understand that its purpose is to validate the areas of success in their program's operation.

You'll want to avoid an evaluation process that overly burdens your staff or that might be too intrusive to your teen participants.

"Ownership by staff is part of any good program evaluation process," Marx said. "Local programs should look at ways to foster the development of in-house evaluation skills. We need to empower the service providers to feel confident about implementing an evaluation process. The tools themselves can be simple. Our message should be, 'Everyone can do it.'"

Developing Statewide Networks

Karen Quebe, co-director of TEXNET, a statewide adolescent pregnancy evaluation project of the Texas Association Concerned with School Age Parenthood (TACSAP) and the University of Texas School of Public Health in Houston, developed the project after hearing similar evaluation concerns expressed by program providers across the state.

Whether from the large programs with million dollar budgets or single staff operations, providers were concerned about the same issues:

- "No one is sharing data."
- "I'm working in isolation."
- "We have no sources for a standard evaluation instrument."
- "We have no way to measure how good our instruments are."
- "We have no basis for a comparison."

Additional program provider frustrations included the pressure from funders to quantify results without providing the appropriate funding for an effective program evaluation process. Quebe continued:

Providers also indicated their concern that funders were reluctant to put money into long-term evaluations. In other words, providers felt that the funders wanted results but were not willing either to wait or to pay.

Program providers feel overwhelmed. They don't know where to start. Those who have started feel the need to show impact results immediately, expecting too much too soon. Program providers must help educate funders about reasonable expectations in terms of results, and what they need to provide to obtain those results.

The majority of the local programs we've talked with across the state are coming in at the ground level. They need help in understanding what's involved in determining an evaluation process and where they should start. Hopefully, the TEXNET project, funded by the Hogg Foundation, will provide the much-needed support for local programs by offering technical assistance in refining individual program evaluation efforts. TEXNET is also creating a statewide network of program evaluators who will be available to assist local programs.

Evaluation—A Priority

Four main issues related to program evaluation are:

1) **Clarity.** Are there clear goals and well defined criteria for success?

2) **Accountability.** Is the data being collected accurate, appropriate, and of a quality that will allow for a clear evaluation of the program?

3) **Effectiveness.** Is there a match between the program's objectives and that which is being measured?

4) **Efficiency.** Is the data being collected in an orderly, appropriate process that is understood and supported by all staff members involved?

Basically, your evaluation method should analyze the status before and after the program's implementation, and compare the resource investment versus the ultimate program results.

Evaluation takes money, time and thought, but done well, the results are worth it.

CHAPTER 10

Marketing Your Message

Marketing in the most basic sense is packaging and promoting a product so someone will buy it—either literally or figuratively. A standard term in the business world, marketing is becoming an increasingly important concept in human services. Marketing involves defining your potential audience; identifying their characteristics; designing an appropriate, appealing message; and developing strategies to deliver the message to the specific individuals or groups identified.

In terms of marketing your adolescent pregnancy prevention or care program, who is your program's target audience? The teens? Absolutely, but you also have other important target audiences—your funding sources, your parent organization, key community leaders, the media, and the community-at-large. Any marketing plan developed by your program should focus on each of these key groups. Never assume that everyone who should, knows about your program. Never miss an opportunity to reinforce your message with client groups.

In addition to program planning and budgeting, you need to have a plan for advocacy and public relations or marketing. If this isn't built into the program, it probably won't be done, or it will have low priority among the things you'll do when you have free time. Marketing your program, however, may be critical to its future success.

Three areas of promotion are essential to teen pregnancy prevention and care programs. All are intertwined, and each needs to be done continuously to maintain a strong base of support:

- **Awareness** — Marketing to funders, the media, the business sector, and the general community.
- **Outreach** — Marketing to the program participants.
- **Advocacy** — Marketing to policy-makers.

Developing Your Message

We live in a world jammed with information where marketing a message on TV has been reduced to thirty-second sound bites. To reach your target audiences with the message, you'll need to develop clear, concise descriptions that capture their interest immediately and project the feeling you want conveyed about your program and its goals. In developing your message, share your vision, then tell the target audience clearly what your program does and why they should become involved, or even care.

The words you use in marketing your program need to be tailored to the self-interests of the specific target audience. Use language that relates to their world. Cost effectiveness and public/private partnership may appeal to the corporate sector because their concern is the bottom line. A message to teens, on the other hand, should stress immediate benefits to them.

Developing Your Materials

In these days of personal computers and desktop publishing, even small programs can develop attractive brochures and other printed materials. A colorful brochure describing the program is important. If you can't afford a slick professionally-produced piece, create the best you can with your resources. Some local print shops have computers and laser printers available for customer use.

Financially constrained programs often have tight printing budgets and make do with quickly typed and inexpensively duplicated promotional materials. Look for individuals or businesses which might provide artwork or printing as an in-kind donation. Local TV or radio stations may be willing to donate assistance in developing public service announcements.

Use flyers or brochures to inform, and distribute them widely. Send them to your school counselors, to social workers, to the staff in counseling agencies, to youth clinics, to doctors' offices, and all places that might make referrals. And don't forget the clergy in your community. They're eager for information which may help a family through a crisis.

Programs which have been in existence a number of years may need to revitalize their image in the community. Simple things such as an updated logo, a new graphic design, a change in accent color, or using more contemporary language may be helpful. Make the review of your materials part of an annual marketing plan.

Send a mailing (with your brochure) offering your services as a guest speaker to PTA presidents, church groups, Rotary Club, Chamber of Commerce, and other local groups. You could develop a short slide or video presentation (with written permission, of course, from the teens shown in the presentation). Be sure to include in your presentation specific ways your program is helping the community, and specific ways they can help your program.

Marketing to Potential Clients

Don't assume the young people who need your services will flock to enroll. Effective outreach (marketing) to potential participants in teen pregnancy prevention and care programs is essential. If there is one young person who needs your services but isn't there because s/he doesn't know about your program, there's room to improve your marketing and outreach.

Marketing to teens involves designing a message and materials that will reach them, and that will be relevant to them.

Everyone receives thousands of messages every day from TV, radio, magazines, store displays, and a variety of other sources. To compete with the barrage of messages teens receive daily, it's critical that program information be presented in a teen-oriented manner and placed where teens will see or hear it. Keep the message simple, clear, non-threatening, and non-judgmental. A teen panel or advisory committee can provide valuable assistance in giving feedback for potential marketing materials.

Develop a poster promoting your program and place it in clinics, doctors' offices, welfare and other social service offices, community centers, unemployment offices, schools (classrooms, counselors, and nurses' offices, cafeteria, physical education areas), anywhere young people might gather. Put the same information on a 3"x5" card and place it on supermarket, laundromat, and other community bulletin boards.

There are many good examples of creative marketing strategies to reach teens with a program's message. **The Coalition on Responsible Parenting and Adolescent Sexuality (C.O.R.P.A.S.),** a service provider coalition in **Dallas, Texas,** prepared a pocket-size listing of programs and services available in the community to help adolescents who are pregnant or facing other problem situations. Copies of the help lists were placed near the check-out counters of local convenience stores.

The **"Let's Talk"** prevention program in **Atlanta, Georgia,** printed small plastic ruler/bookmarks for distribution in the schools. One side of the bookmark listed "Three Simple Ways to Say No." The other side said, "If you need us, call us. Teen Services Program, (phone number)."

During **"Let's Talk"** month in **Charlotte, North Carolina,** many of the physicians who work with children or youth wore buttons that said, "I'm an Askable Doc," indicating they were ready and willing to talk with young people or their families about adolescent sexuality issues.

The Adolescent Pregnancy Coalition in **Maine** developed a marketing theme for a recent statewide conference. One of the prevention marketing tools developed by the state coalition for distribution to teens throughout the state by local community programs is a plastic "credit card." On the front the card reads,

"Fast Forward." The back side lists seven things the teenager can take credit for, as a person in control of his/her life. The bottom of the card has a signature strip where the teen can sign as the "Credit Holder."

A good source of publicity for reaching teens is your local school newspaper. The kids read them, and it's the kids who need to be reached. Perhaps a student reporter would do a series on the prevention of too-early pregnancy, focusing on your program but written in their words for their peers.

The school newspaper might also run an ad such as the one placed by the **Tracy Teen Mother Program (TMP),** ABC Unified School District, **Cerritos, California:**

Do You Know Someone
YOUNG AND PREGNANT?

**The ABC Unified School District
TEEN MOTHER PROGRAM
can help her!**
Tracy Education Center
12222 Cuesta, Cerritos, CA 90701   213/926-5566

A nurse in the above district found a particularly effective spot for Teen Mother Program brochures—inside the door of the restroom in her office. Pregnant students not yet broadcasting their pregnancy tended to be there occasionally. With the brochures she put white envelopes so the student could take the brochure without advertising the fact of her pregnancy.

Telephone Is Marketing Tool

How staff responds to telephone calls is an important part of marketing to potential clients. If a staff member is willing, put her/his home phone number in addition to the agency number on posters, brochures, and other promotion items.

Pat Alviso, coordinator of the Tracy Teen Mother Program, puts her home telephone number on all outreach materials. She doesn't get a lot of calls at home, but says those she receives are important. A pregnant teen may have the courage to make only one phone call before giving up, and that one effort may not be made during office hours.

"When a client calls, it's important to bend over backwards in responding," Alviso stressed. "First, make her feel welcome and wanted. Explain the program. Be concerned. Above all, get her name and phone number. If she hangs up, you may never hear from her again."

Alviso strongly recommends home visits for potential pregnant and parenting clients. "Her self-esteem may be almost non-existent, and her family may think no one wants to help. A home visit, preferably including her parents and/or husband/boyfriend can express your concern and your eagerness to help better than any phone call or office visit," she concluded.

Follow-up of clients after they leave your program offers several advantages. First, they may need your support. Second, they can be your best referral sources. An additional advantage is the evaluation possibilities of a well-managed follow-up.

The Tracy TMP teachers have an annual TMP alumna potluck supper. Included with the invitation to the supper is a questionnaire which is changed each year, but is always designed to obtain crucial information about respondents' continuing education, childbirth, jobs, and other personal items. Along with a self-addressed stamped envelope is a promise to include in the next year's letter information obtained from the questionnaire. Response is good, according to Alviso.

Marketing to the Community

Marketing to the community must be constant, and can be done effectively through existing community groups in a variety of ways.

Always being available to talk about teen pregnancy issues and about your program is important. Let your churches, PTAs, and other community organizations know you're willing to speak at their meetings. Volunteer to talk with school personnel. Not only counselors and nurses, but also teachers and administrators need to know about your services.

Some teen parent program teachers send newsletters periodically to all school district staff. The same technique would be helpful in social service agencies and health centers which offer special programs for young people.

Plan an open house and invite more people than you think you can handle. Many won't come, but your well-designed invitation can give them information about your program. Even if they don't come, they may remember your services. This may have benefits for future referrals or in simply making your program more visible.

Lady Pitts School, Milwaukee, Wisconsin, was started in 1968. Recently, to reinforce community support, Principal Peggy Clapp helped write a White Paper describing the incidence and costs of adolescent pregnancy and parenting in Milwaukee as a means of gaining broad-based support from the community for adolescent pregnancy prevention efforts.

The paper was distributed at a session of the Milwaukee Education Roundtable, a group which meets several times during the year with community leaders to discuss specific educational problems along with strategic options, conclusions, and recommendations.

Clapp commented:

> *We explained to the community that teen pregnancy and parenting is not just a teen and parent concern, but a whole community's concern. The business community looks at their pocketbooks, so we stressed the financial impact of teen pregnancy. We talked about teen parents being at risk for costly abnormal deliveries, for having children with medical problems, for dropping out of school and not being able to find a job, and about their need for child care.*
>
> *The Education Roundtable includes not only school people, but also foundation representatives, the mayor's office, health and human service providers, ministers, and other community people.*
>
> *The schools and agencies know they can't do it alone. We have to let the community know what it means to them, what our programs are facing, and what we need from each of them.*

Developing a Marketing Network

Since most programs don't have funds for a professional PR
person, it's important to develop a marketing network. Schools,
youth agencies, and other key groups in the community should
know about your program and become part of your marketing
network. Identify people who have contact with youth—counselors, teachers, coaches, nurses, and secretaries at school;
church youth group leaders; youth agency staff; volunteer
groups; local businesses that employ young people; and community hotlines. Plan to visit with these people and programs
personally, especially when new people are hired.

A presentation at a school faculty meeting will reach the
teachers and clarify the purpose of your program. Other groups
will have meetings where you can present information and
recruit their assistance in promoting the program or making
referrals.

An Advisory Council can become the core of a local
program's marketing network by having their role include
promoting the program in the community. They can also help
counter negative publicity if it occurs.

Sue Dolezal, **Teen Renaissance, Brighton, Colorado,**
coordinates a school-based program for pregnant and parenting
teens and their children. She described the support provided by
the program's advisory committee:

> *Members of the advisory committee have been active
> in promoting the program in the community. They devel-
> oped a slide/tape presentation of Teen Renaissance, and
> in doing so, became closer to the girls in the program.
> This in turn solidified their support.*
>
> *The advisory committee members weren't service
> provider people. Rather, we had the powerful people—
> representatives from Chamber of Commerce, Kiwanis,
> and Rotary, a physician, an attorney, religious leaders,
> and some people from the local hospital. We had
> leaders from the Hispanic community and a school
> board member who called up and said she wanted to be
> on the committee.*

They spoke to several service clubs in our commu-
nity, and they held an open house so people could see
what we were doing. They put articles in the paper and
did the behind-the-scenes things to help us gain commu-
nity support and to build awareness.

Raising public awareness of the incidence and risks of teen
pregnancy and of prevention efforts means marketing your
issue. Sometimes this becomes the major focus of an organization. Barbara Huberman, chairperson, North Carolina Coalition
on Adolescent Pregnancy, (NCCAP) sees their role as the
"keeper of awareness." She said, "We must constantly be the
agency who tells the community that adolescent pregnancy is a
problem. We do this through local TV shows, conferences,
newsletters, media campaigns, and program presentations. We
must be an advocate for a population that has no advocate."

Marketing to Funders

Sometimes even well-planned and well-run adolescent
pregnancy programs lose funding, community support, and teen
participants because they do not continuously market their
program to each of these groups. This is especially true with
funding. Programs receiving local financial support from city or
county agencies, foundations, businesses, churches, service
organizations, or other community groups must constantly sell
themselves and the value of their existence to individuals in
leadership positions.

Program personnel must constantly emphasize the impact the
program is having on the lives of young people in the community. They must also stress the importance to the life of the
program of support from the funders.

Be sure to follow the policies of your funding sources. Send
them your newsletters. If they are local, initiate regular formal
and informal contact with them. Keep them informed! If major
problems occur, alert your funding source early. No one likes to
be the last to know about a problem. Being up-front lets your
supporters in on the problem-solving process which can work
toward building ownership and commitment.

Marketing to the Business Sector

It is particularly important to watch your language when
marketing your program to members of the business sector of
your community. Words, phrases, and acronyms that are common and clearly understood in social service circles may be a
foreign language in the business world. Don't assume the business community has no interest in your program, and don't
assume business community members are unapproachable. Do,
however, understand their interests and standard ways of operation when you target your message to this group.

The business community usually will be concerned about
your issues and program for reasons related to their own self
interest. They want to know what supporting or investing in
your program will mean to them. They want to know if their
involvement is a cost-effective investment. They don't have
time to waste, and it is important to get to the bottom line
quickly.

Some parts of the business community may not want to deal
with sexuality and pregnancy issues. However, they are vitally
interested in an educated, literate, and skilled labor force. They
want to reduce the number of people dependent on the welfare
system, and they may be willing to invest resources in cost-
effective programs with a positive return.

Ask for advice from members of the business community
when you develop a marketing activity targeting that group. One
place to start might be the corporate members on the local
United Way Board of Directors. They should already be sensitized to the general human service needs of the community and
committed to the investment of corporate resources in
implementing program responses.

Marketing Through the Media

"It pays to advertise" may not seem appropriate for teen
pregnancy programs—but it is. People don't want to know about
programs for pregnant and parenting teens—until their daughter
or best friend's daughter is pregnant. If they've read a feature
story about the program in their local paper, they're far more
likely to remember there's help when they need it.

Send press releases regularly to your local papers and other media. Topics might be a staff change in your program, the beginning of a new semester of services, classroom speakers, or feature stories about clients who are doing well in spite of obstacles.

Take advantage of opportunities to promote a positive program image through local newspaper articles or TV or radio programs. Plan your media coverage carefully. If you're involving teens in media interviews, prepare them adequately for the experience. An interview can be intimidating for an adult, and extremely so for a young person who may be asked abruptly by the interviewer to share very personal facts about her life.

Directors of some adolescent pregnancy prevention and care programs have decided, through experience, to have adult staff or board members handle all interviews with the media to avoid any unnecessary embarrassment, hurt feelings, or exploitation of the young people in the program. However, some teens thoroughly enjoy media opportunities. They, preferably with an adult staff member also involved, can provide the positive human interest kind of story both your program supporters and the media appreciate.

When a reporter calls, have a quick list of positive information to share. Are young people verbalizing a desire to delay pregnancy until they're ready to parent? Are they setting goals for themselves, then working toward those goals?

If you work with pregnant and parenting teens, how many of the young mothers are graduating from high school because of the support provided by the program? How many return to school because of the special program? Tell the reporter. Have a clear idea of the message you want reported and keep repeating it. Most reporters will follow your direction.

Make sure your data and information are clear and accurate. Have printed fact sheets and descriptive information about your program available for a reporter to use in preparing an article. Practice difficult subject areas ahead of time so you have smooth, genuine responses that are comfortable and appropriate. Just remember, working with the media is a learned skill that improves with experience.

Look for positive ways to involve the local media directly in what you're doing. Get to know the reporter or reporters who cover your issue for the local media. Send them copies of your newsletters and regular press releases about events. Ask for their advice and assistance. Put a representative from the media on your Advisory Board.

See Appendix, page 237, "Managing the Media: A Fifteen-Step Plan" by Howard Klink, Public Affairs Director, Multnomah County Department of Human Services, Portland, Oregon.

Finding Media Materials

Prize-winning reproducible advertisements stressing the prevention of teen pregnancy are available from the International Newspaper Advertising and Marketing Executives Foundation (INAME), Reston, Virginia. The American Academy of Advertising/INAME Foundation sponsors an annual newspaper advertising competition for college advertising and marketing students. The 1988-1989 contest focused on ads for the prevention of teenage pregnancy.

National winners were chosen from more than 2,300 entries. The collection of ads available for use in *Newspaper Advertising Student Competition 1988-1989* includes three complete national winning ad series, and a sample ad from each of the thirty-three regional winning series and honorable mentions. These ads may be adapted for local use and used as long as a copy of the adapted ad is sent to the professor whose student created the ad. Contact the NOAPP office for more information.

A recent creative marketing project to promote early prenatal care in Washington, DC, is an awareness and incentive campaign called "Beautiful Babies Right from the Start" involving media as a primary sponsor. A collaborative effort of the **March of Dimes, Blue Cross and Blue Shield of the National Capital Area,** and **WRC-TV/Channel 4,** the local NBC affiliate, the campaign is a response to the area's consistently high incidence of low birthweight babies, a high percentage of whom are born to teenagers.

The multi-media educational campaign includes television documentaries, news stories, editorials, public service announcements by well-known celebrities, direct mail outreach, and even door-to-door contact.

The campaign also includes an incentive program which provides coupon books for services and products useful during pregnancy and the child's first year of life. By involving a corporate sponsor and a local TV station, the March of Dimes gained valuable financial and media resources in marketing its prenatal care campaign.

Importance of Marketing Plan

Every adolescent pregnancy program interacts with a number of target audiences that potentially affect the organization— clients, the community, funders, media, business sector, and policy-makers. Each of these audiences has a reason to be involved with the program and has resources to share.

A well-developed marketing plan, incorporating appropriate messages for each identified target audience, is necessary to communicate effectively the program's benefits and ensure each group's continued support and involvement.

CHAPTER 11

Advocating To Policy-Makers

Most service providers are client advocates, a role they understand and feel competent to handle—although it can be a frustrating and emotionally draining experience. Where service providers are less comfortable and less successful is moving from the individual client advocacy to the system advocacy level.

Karen Pittman, Clearinghouse Director, Children's Defense Fund, says, "By the time the seventeenth kid has come in the door with the same problem, and a repeating pattern emerges, we need to bump up a level in terms of our advocacy. This can be difficult for service providers. It's hard to find time to work on the 'holes in the system' on a larger advocacy scale." It also may seem too overwhelming a task to tackle.

Nevertheless, Kate Hanley, Community Relations Director, Arizona Family Planning Council, stresses that advocacy should be a major part of an adolescent pregnancy prevention and care program's activities. She said:

*Policy-makers want to be responsive to their constitu-
ents. We need to be sure, as advocates for young people,
that we take our message to them because we're the ones
with the information. That message needs to be clear, they
need to hear it, and we must hold them accountable. It's
real PR work, and it needs to be done at all levels.*

Advocacy Versus Lobbying

Many local adolescent pregnancy programs fall into the non-
profit, tax-exempt 501(c)(3) category under the Internal Revenue Service code. This type of organization needs to understand
clearly the guidelines that govern its advocacy activities.

Local program providers and their volunteer board members
have an important role to play in educating public officials about
adolescent pregnancy issues. Certainly organizations can and
should share information about their program, the needs of their
client population, and related funding or policy issues with the
appropriate elected and appointed officials and their staff
members. They need to develop an on-going relationship with
the key staff members who handle human service issues.

Beyond educating public officials about their program and its
needs, non-profit, tax-exempt organizations are able to participate in many kinds of public affairs and public policy activities,
but not in others.

In general, staff and volunteers as representatives of a non-
profit, tax-exempt organization:

- **CAN:** Educate candidates and the public about adolescent
  pregnancy issues and concerns.
  Share information about specific legislation.

- **CANNOT:** Endorse candidates for elective office.
  Participate in campaigns or give organizational support
  such as use of facility or allowing purchase of
  organization's mailing list for campaign purposes.
  Spend more than a designated percent of their operating
  budget on lobbying activities to promote a particular piece
  of legislation.

Additionally, specific funding sources may have limits on the type of advocacy your program can perform. Know those limitations, and if you have questions, discuss them in advance with the funding source.

A program's staff and volunteers are free as individuals to endorse, work for, and/or make contributions to candidates on their own time as long as it is clear that they are not acting in their capacity as representatives of the organization.

Advocacy Begins at Home

Advocacy can begin with your organization's board members and administrators. As advocates for the teen pregnancy prevention continuum, you're concerned about a wide range of issues and need to articulate those issues: prenatal care, general health care for young people, child care, homelessness, paternity issues, child support, youth employment, educational opportunities, welfare reform—all of these are our issues. Don't assume your program's board and administrators know all about all these issues. Have a briefing before any meeting with policy-makers.

Elected and appointed people in your city and county make decisions about local funding, program development, or policies. These decision-makers need to be shown the diversity of our issues. Hanley commented:

> *Get the word OUT. For example, invite these decision-makers to an open house or graduation or for special-interest evenings. Send information about the numbers we're serving, the success stories we have, the problems and challenges some of our kids are facing.*
>
> *Keep in mind that we're not the only ones carrying the message. The best advocates are those we serve, the families of the kids.*
>
> *When we invite candidates to our schools or when we're part of a forum, we need to ask pointed and specific questions about our issues. "Would you support funding for a teen pregnancy program?" Get them on record taking this favorable position by sending a follow-up letter*

*Paquin Alternative School student
testifies at Congressional hearing.*

saying, "This is what I understand you said. Thank you."
At the same time, we must make a list of the unfavorable
positions they're taking. Our challenge is to share
information that will help them change that position.

Sometimes these people may seem intimidating to
program providers because they've been elected to a
public office. Keep in mind they're regular folks who have
worked hard in a career that's different from ours, a
political career. Now they're in positions where they must
make important decisions that impact all of us, yet we're
the experts with the information. They actually need our
input to make careful and informed decisions. We must
realize how valuable and important our information is to
these elected officials. We don't want them to make
decisions in a vacuum. We need to be a resource for them.

Use the words of your clients in your advocacy efforts.
If you get a particularly insightful comment from a
student, ask the student if it's okay to share the comment
with others. These words and feelings will touch others as
much as they touch us.

If you send this to elected officials, they get a better
idea of who these kids are, and of the growth that's taking
place in our programs. Sometimes we overlook how
valuable our clients' personal testimony is. They're our
best public relations resource.

Being a Resource for Policy-makers

People often assume that policy-makers are knowledgeable
about a particular subject. Mary Polk, former member of the
Texas House of Representatives, stressed that no policy-maker
can be knowledgeable about everything.

You need to be a resource for your local and state policy-
makers. Find someone who knows the policy-maker, someone
who can sit down with him/her, establish a relationship, and help
the policy-maker become an expert in the field. Polk recommends saying, "When this subject comes up, I'd be happy to
give you information on it, collect stats, do anything I can to
help you when you have to make a decision on this subject."

Many policy-makers appreciate this kind of help, according to
Polk, because they don't have time to develop background
knowledge in everything.

Polk became interested in teenage pregnancy when a group in
El Paso asked, "How do we get involved?" She explained:

> *They educated me, and it became a real partnership.*
> *That's what you have to do. You aren't going to find all*
> *the members of the Legislature interested in the subject. If*
> *one person isn't interested, find somebody else. You don't*
> *need all those legislators. All you need is a majority.*
>
> *You also need to get other groups of people together*
> *who are interested in your issue—the schools, parents,*
> *pediatricians—all those whose lives are touched by teen*
> *pregnancy. Get a wide spectrum of people to give their*
> *viewpoints, each a little different from yours. Legislators*
> *want to hear it's not just a special interest thing.*
>
> *If you can make a legislator look good to colleagues or*
> *to the constituency back home, you're ahead. The more*
> *support you give them, the better they'll respond to your*
> *request for help, whether it's for funding or to change a*
> *policy.*
>
> *Remember to thank your legislator for help even if your*
> *bill doesn't get passed this session. Sometimes it takes*
> *several sessions to get a piece of legislation through.*
>
> *You follow exactly the same process whether you're in*
> *a tiny town or in a big city. You're going to have to*
> *educate that legislator because s/he will have to carry the*
> *legislation. You can testify, but it's the legislator who will*
> *have to carry the legislation.*

Linda Larason, Oklahoma State Representative, District 88,
remembers being timid about talking with legislators:

> *Several years ago, when I was active in the League of*
> *Women Voters, I was terribly intimidated by the prospect*
> *of talking to my representative and senator or, heaven*
> *forbid, at the idea of going to the Capitol to lobby the*

entire body. Since being elected to office, I have trouble believing I was ever scared to carry my message to the statehouse! And I forget that other people may not be comfortable talking with me.

Because Larason feels it is vitally important for those who care about children to educate policy-makers regarding the need for specific legislation for good programs, she offered some suggestions:

Tips for Advocating on Teen Pregnancy Issues

Know your subject. You should feel comfortable with it, but don't be embarrassed to admit you may not know the answer to a specific question. Offer to find the information and forward it. And always be honest. If your credibility is ever questioned, you won't regain it. Remember, our careers are on the line, and we must be able to defend our votes.

Know as much as possible about the individual policy-maker you're meeting. Is s/he married? With children? What ages? Any birth defects, handicaps, young deaths, etc., in the family that are public knowledge? (If so, you'll likely find a sympathetic ear to the cause you're supporting.) What kinds of legislation has s/he authored?

Remember that most representatives/senators will, no doubt, pay closer (and quicker) attention to someone from his or her own district. That's not to say that you can't get the ear of someone else if you're representing an organization or a specific piece of legislation, but even then it's helpful to get someone from the home district to reinforce your position.

Remember that schedules are difficult to follow during a legislative session. Committee meetings run past appointed times, other people may have dropped in just minutes before your scheduled appointment and stayed, meetings may be called on the spur of the moment. Be prepared for that, and don't take it as a personal rebuff.

If you're not able to schedule an appointment, or if it gets interrupted or postponed, leave materials, if possible, with a

personal note. Offer to come back, or ask the representative/
senator to call you.

Find a way to personalize your message. We are inundated
with reading materials and statistics. If your county had enough
teen births during the past five years to fill the football stadium,
make that fact known.

Take someone with you if you feel uncomfortable.

**Unless this is a priority issue with the legislator, you'll
know more about it than s/he does.** Provide information
without making the receiver feel inadequate for not knowing the
facts.

Do your homework. Find an interested and appropriate
person to ask about the piece of legislation you need authored. Is
that legislator interested, articulate, respected, and trusted by
other members? Sometimes an author who is considered too
liberal or too conservative can torpedo a good piece of
legislation without study or debate.

Remember that you can't win 'em all. There will be disap-
pointments, but often you can win the second or third time
around.

Don't be frightened. There is absolutely no reason to be. If a
particular legislator is rude, abrupt, or downright nasty to you,
that's not your problem—it's the legislator's.

Thank your supporters. This should be self-evident. The
simple courtesy of a "Thank you" goes a long way and will be
remembered the next time you contact the individual.

Advocating and Building State Initiatives

Constancia Warren, Director of Adolescent Pregnancy
Programs for the Center for Public Advocacy Research, stresses
that by becoming known as the technical expert in the field, you
become the expert policy-makers count on for information. She
suggests a three-pronged approach to advocacy, an approach
based on her experience shaping New York State policy on
school-based clinics (SBCs).

Warren's suggestions, designed specifically for advocates for
SBCs, provide valuable guidance for advocates of policies in
support of services for young people, wherever those services

may fit on the teen pregnancy prevention continuum. Warren's guidelines were featured in *Clinic News* (Support Center for School-Based Clinics), Winter, 1989, pages 8-9:

Step 1: Research

Research involves both building a knowledge base and providing a basis for a campaign. Advocates should develop a report that includes a description of the program, the history of the situation in the state, and documentation of the need. Specific, accurate demographic data is essential in the research stage. It is also essential to include recommendations on implementation plans and funding sources, existing and potential.

Incidentally the research process brings advocates into contact with potential constituents as well as decision makers. Some aspects of research create relationships that will be valuable in later advocacy efforts.

Step 2: Constituency

The second step in the process is constituency building. Advocates can initiate informal coalitions by forming working groups to study particular issues. These groups pull in key players—members of organizations with shared concerns, community leaders, constituents—to identify issues, plan strategy, delegate tasks, explore problems, and plan activities to broaden the base.

Advocates should also participate in other groups, both to support their own issues there and to get their issues onto others' agendas if they aren't already.

Another element in constituency building is organizing public events. Legislative hearings provide excellent opportunities to spread the message.

In addition, events like the "Youth Speak Out" held in New York can be enormously powerful. For this occasion, children in schools with SBCs were carefully selected to speak on what SBCs meant in their lives. Policy-makers, parents, the community, and the press were invited to attend. The meeting was timed to get press coverage right before the school board considered the issue of clinics in the schools.

Step 3: Working with Decision Makers

The final step in successful advocacy is working with decision makers. Legislators, or more often, their staff are important allies. Much of the work involved in moving through a specific agenda, however, is not legislation but is, rather, regulation, interpretation, and implementation. In these efforts, agency staff are crucial allies. Executive branch staff are also important in facilitating legislative and agency activities.

Warren noted that there are many types of interaction with decision makers in addition to direct advocacy. Advocates should share information with decision makers and gather information from them. They should assist in identifying resources for funding, for expert testimony, and for hearing agendas. They should assist in the negotiations among legislators and administrators as they develop policy. Finally, advocates should "broker," that is, bring together decision makers at different levels of state government, in different agencies.

Warren emphasized that all of these efforts bear fruit, although in many cases it takes years to see the results.

Advocacy—The Bottom Line

Whether talking with a local school board member or your Congressional representative, two basic issues each policy-maker will be concerned with are: Does it work? How much does it cost?

Policy-makers work on and respond to a multitude of issues at any given time. To keep your issue a priority for their attention, make sure you have:

• **A clear, consistent message** that documents your program success and cost effectiveness.

• **A plan for keeping policy-makers informed** about your program in an on-going manner.

Visit them and invite them to visit your program. Send them newsletters and reports. Send them press releases about your program's activities and copies of news articles. Get to know their staff members on a first name basis. Advocacy involves constant educating, nurturing, and encouraging policy-makers to become involved with adolescent pregnancy issues.

CHAPTER 12

Maintaining Success

Now you have identified a need for an adolescent pregnancy prevention or care program in your community and you have planned a program to respond to that need. The program has or will have a clear mission and goals, a structure, specific content, a location, local support, and funding for at least an initial period of time.

At this point, it is critical to consider seriously some issues important not only in building, but in *maintaining* a successful future for the program.

Young people don't vote, they aren't active advocates for their needs, and they often are a tough client population to reach and serve. Too often, adolescent pregnancy prevention and care programs are the first to go when the funding cuts occur. Thus, programs serving young people, and particularly at-risk young people, need to place a high priority on factors that will ensure both short-term success and long-term survival.

Building a Business-Like Board

Whether your program is operated under the direction of an informal committee or a formal board of directors, strong leadership must be continually recruited and trained for effective program planning and implementation. In the beginning, the administrative group may be formed as an informal committee which includes many of the people who gathered the data, presented the case, designed the program content, and initiated the actual program. Often a small and close-knit group, these people have a personal attachment to the program as it is, figuratively speaking, "their baby."

As the program grows and matures over time, the group administering the program will likewise go through various developmental stages. Policies and procedures for the operation of both the program and the administrative group may need to become more formalized.

You may need to recruit new people who bring additional skills and contact networks to the program. You may need to develop a committee structure to handle specific functions such as fundraising and special events.

The board is responsible for ensuring the integrity and effectiveness of the organization. Basic functions of a board will be:

- **Financial accountability**
- **Legal responsibility**
- **Organizational management**
- **Fundraising and long-term financial development**
- **Maintaining the organization's identity**
- **Keeping the mission alive**

To build a strong, business-like board for your program, it is important to:

- **Assess what type of organization you *are*.**
- **Assess what type of board you *have*.**
- **Assess what type of board you *want*.**
- **Design a leadership development plan to meet your program's *needs*.**

The leadership development plan for a board of directors should:

- **Develop board selection criteria**—what range of skills are needed?
- **Specify board responsibilities**—assign meaningful duties and hold members accountable.
- **Specify employed/volunteer staff responsibilities**—clarify roles, expectations, and lines of accountability.
- **Seek ways for the board members to receive initial and recurrent training**—opportunities for growth.
- **Prepare/amend bylaws as necessary**—to keep the process efficient and effective.
- **Review annually**—to revise and alter as needed.

Board members are volunteers who are interested in your program and willing to give their time and their skills to help. They need to be used effectively.

Clarifying expectations regarding their role, responsibilities, and time commitments prior to beginning their tenure on the board will help orient them and reduce the possibility of confused expectations later on.

Good communication is vital. Regularly scheduled meetings with meaningful agendas that are sent to the board members in advance are important to the efficient operation of a board of directors. People want to be prepared for the discussion and decision-making at the meeting.

Tasks that don't require the attention of the full board can be given to ad hoc groups or committees for consideration. Committees need to receive clearly defined tasks, adequate timelines to complete their assignments, and appropriate staff support.

Board members need to be treated as professionals. Respect their input and try to avoid wasting their time. Recognize that there will be situations where legitimate areas of disagreement may arise as the board carries out its work. Set a tone that respects everyone's opinion yet resolves those disagreements in a manner that will not be destructive to the program.

Establishing Advisory Council

Some programs may have both a working board of directors that carries out the on-going program operation and a separate advisory group. The latter group is often composed of influential, highly visible community leaders whose names, contacts, or access to resources within the community are valuable to the program. Sometimes the group will be asked to help with specific issues or activities such as fundraising.

Whether the program is part of an existing organization or a totally new program, an advisory committee can be established to help plan, administer, evaluate, and promote the program within the organization and within the community. This will increase the program's recognition as an important part of the community, and will create a group of individuals who can serve as resources for the program in multiple ways.

People with critical expertise such as doctors, lawyers, and city council members who would be unable to commit a great deal of time to the program may be interested in serving in an advisory capacity. Don't assume these people aren't interested. Ask them to serve, but be specific as to exactly what their role would be.

New Futures School, Albuquerque, New Mexico, started in a church basement in 1971 with four students. Today, three hundred pregnant and parenting teens attend New Futures in a $1.7 million building planned to meet their specific needs. Caroline Gaston, principal during most of New Future's existence, credits much of the program's success to the work of the New Futures Board of Directors:

> *Our advisory councils function under the board. They report back at the board meetings. Our bylaws say we meet six times a year, but generally it's eight. We're a broad-based board representing the religious community, parents of students and former students, business people, health people, and interested community volunteers. We want to be sure they are people who are interested in our issue. We look for people who can be our eyes and ears and voices in the community.*
>
> *One aspect of the New Futures program is usually reviewed at each meeting. Sometimes we look at issues of teen parenting beyond New Futures School. We always seem to stay terribly terribly busy.*

*We set aside one board meeting each year where we
hear from students. Lately we've sponsored an annual
decision-makers luncheon. Each member of the Board
invites community leaders, legislators, school board
members, and others. At that luncheon, we have students
as the spokespeople, and they're very effective at getting
our purpose across to our guests.*

*In addition to our community based board, we have
advisory committees including our vocational advisory
group and special advisory committees from time to
time as we need them. We had a special building advisory committee when our new facility was being con-
structed. When we started the children's literature
program, we were concerned that it should represent the
various ethnic groups in our culture. We wanted not
only reading but children's rhymes, singing, and games,
so we had a four-culture advisory committee.*

*It's terribly time-consuming to be responsive to all
these groups. If they want a speaker for their meetings,
you either speak or send somebody else. You have to be
visible in the community. And you can't just be interested in your issue and hope that these people will come
along. You also have to be interested in their issues and
serve on their boards. We've had New Futures people
on at least seven different community advisory groups.*

*Several of us go out regularly doing presentations.
We usually have one-page handouts that describe
quickly and concisely what we're doing and the results.*

Long-Range Planning

Day-to-day concerns are often all-consuming for the staff and
volunteers working with an adolescent pregnancy care or
prevention program. However, from the beginning, energy must
be focused on a formalized long-range planning process. While
having a long-range plan does not guarantee the absence of
crises, it does provide direction for the program and its supporters. It is your road map into the future, making it easier to figure
out how to get from your present situation to your ultimate goal.

A long-range plan articulates your needs for the future operation and expansion of the program and identifies the resources that will be required along the way. Different future scenarios can be examined and planned in advance, so the program is prepared for various contingencies that might arise. A long-range plan also gives other agencies and the community at large a sense of where your program is headed.

To develop a long-range plan, you may wish to use resources in the community with planning expertise such as the United Way, corporate volunteers, or individuals involved with local planning departments or task forces. As you develop your long-range plan, you'll explore external factors impacting on the problem your program addresses, such as population trends or the projected economic climate of your community. Looking at the problem and planning your program over a future period of time may give you ideas for changes in policies needed at the local or state level. As patterns emerge which affect policy development, you may need help in bringing this to the attention of the appropriate local or state decision makers.

Long range planning may be tied to future target dates or more broadly tied to levels of future accomplishment. The latter may be more realistic since it is often difficult to predict when growth or funding will actually be achieved.

Nurturing Community Support

New adolescent pregnancy prevention and care programs are being established across the country each year. The biggest challenge ahead comes in sustaining these programs and community initiatives after the current wave of public interest and heightened awareness subsides. There is always the potential for a shift to other issues of funding and program priorities that would compete for scarce resources in the future.

Long-range planning, evaluation, marketing, on-going funding and resource development, and having a contingency plan for coping with cutbacks are important pieces of the safety net needed for a program to last over time. Along with these items, it's important constantly to nurture community-wide support for your program.

To build a broad base of local support, many successful adolescent pregnancy care and prevention programs tie their program efforts to a number of other youth-related activities and issues in the community. By linking adolescent pregnancy efforts with a reduction in child abuse, substance abuse, unemployment, school dropout, birth defects, infant mortality, sexual abuse, welfare dependency, poverty, and poor nutrition, a program can greatly multiply its base of potential supporters. By linking the program effort with increased self-sufficiency, parenting skills, employability, and maternal/child health, the program automatically generates the support and good will of many individuals and organizations.

Successful programs have placed a heavy emphasis on networking, interagency coordination and cooperation, and building a strong base of community support. Dorothy Rothrock, former director of the alternative school program, Continuing Education for Young Families, Kalamazoo, Michigan, says, "If someone is starting an adolescent pregnancy program at this time, my advice is to begin by building broad community support for the concept, then identifying existing community resources—human and financial. I'd also suggest developing a plan for inter-agency cooperation from the beginning to provide the full range of services that pregnant and parenting teens are going to need."

Mary Ann Liebert, NOAPP president and Executive Director of the Washington Alliance Concerned with School Age Parents (WACSAP) says, "Collaboration is the key to long-term success for local adolescent pregnancy prevention and care programs. There is a role for every part of the community to play in addressing the difficult and complex issues related to adolescent pregnancy. Few programs or groups have the resources or capability to provide a fully comprehensive prevention or care program on their own. Effective local program delivery involves a great deal of communication, coordination, and constant planning. It's through collaboration that local programs can maximize their efforts."

In the *Ounce of Prevention Magazine,* Irving Harris, Chairman of the Pittway Corporation Charitable Foundation and

President of the Board of Directors and guiding spirit for the
Ounce of Prevention Fund, shared a story that he felt illustrates
one aspect of prevention:

*A group of individuals were enjoying a picnic along-
side a small stream of rather fast-flowing water. In the
midst of the fun, someone shouted, "There's a child out in
the stream and he's yelling for help." One of the picnick-
ers quickly took off his shoes and trousers and rushed into
the river in time to catch the child and bring him safely to
shore.*

*Just as he was beginning to catch his breath, someone
yelled again, "There's a child in the middle of the
stream." The man rushed into the water again and successfully retrieved the second child.*

*And just as he was sitting down to start to put on his
trousers and shoes again, someone yelled, "There's
another child out there."*

*Somewhat angrily, he said, "Someone else go in this
time," and someone else did.*

*In the meantime, he dressed quickly, put his shoes on,
and started to walk quickly away. Someone said, "Where
are you going in such a rush?"*

*He yelled back, "I'm going up around the bend to see
who is pushing the kids into the river."*

His example illustrates very clearly the bigger problem that
looms on the horizon when addressing adolescent pregnancy
prevention and care programs at any level.

Today our society is "pushing a lot of kids into that river." To
get a handle on adolescent pregnancy, it is imperative that in
local community settings and beyond, we take a hard look at the
conditions that lead to early sexual activity and limited life
options.

We must look for creative ways to bring young people and
families out of a life of poverty and give them a sense of hope, a
sense of dignity, and opportunities to achieve their potential. To
do this, policies must be developed, beginning at the local level,
which support primary prevention and the accessibility of health
care, education, social services, and recreation for everyone.

Keeping the Vision Alive

Starting an adolescent pregnancy prevention or care program is a challenging task. Maintaining and continuing to build the program over time can be equally as challenging. The clients change, staff changes, community attitudes and resources may change, the economic climate for funding may change, and other issues may replace adolescent pregnancy as a priority concern within the administering organization.

Maintaining success requires the ability to adapt to both anticipated and unanticipated changes within the organization and community. Maintaining success requires changing liabilities into assets and challenges into opportunities.

The programs included in this book show but a sampling of the many ways groups in local communities are providing successful adolescentpregnancy prevention and care activities. They have identified a need in their communities and pulled together resources to meet that need. What works in Bangor, Maine, may be different than the programs that prove successful in San Antonio, Texas, or a small community in Kansas.

In every community there is a need for more coordinated, comprehensive approaches in providing adolescent pregnancy programs. Adolescence is a difficult time for young people in our society today. Simply being there, listening, and caring are possibly the most important factors in programs successfully serving teens. A flyer listing programs available at The Door in New York City states that it is "A place to get help . . . A place to get it together . . . A place to be together." That says a lot to teens.

In planning a prevention or care program for your local community, simply start where you are. Even the large comprehensive programs started small. The most important thing is to start with your vision, start somewhere on the adolescent pregnancy prevention continuum, and start helping kids—*now*.

Putting Guidelines Into Practice

Project Redirection, El Paso, Texas, is a county-wide comprehensive program for pregnant and parenting teens which includes a prevention component. It is a wonderful example of the concepts discussed in *Teen Pregnancy Challenge, Book One: Strategies for Change*—building community support, planning the program and defining content, considering the setting, finding diversified funding, evaluating effectiveness, marketing, and maintaining success.

Project Redirection also includes in its prevention and care components many of the program features discussed in *Teen Pregnancy Challenge, Book Two: Programs for Kids*—case management, comprehensive services for pregnant and parenting teens, child care in day care homes and in school centers, use of volunteers, mentors, peer counseling, teen father involvement, and dropout retrieval.

Project Redirection's story was written by its co-founder, Betty Dodson. It is included here as a model of a truly comprehensive program developed over time to meet the needs of young people in El Paso, Texas.

El Paso, Texas—Project Redirection Meeting a Community's Needs

By Betty Dodson, Co-Founder and Former Director

Project Redirection is a large, county-wide program administered by the YWCA of El Paso, Texas, and funded primarily by the Texas Department of Human Services. It grew out of an established alternative education program known as the **School-age Parent Center (SPC)** which was begun in 1974 by the El Paso Independent School District to meet the educational needs of pregnant students in that school district.

In the state of Texas, pregnant students are one of the designated special education categories. Thus they are entitled to state special education funding which offers some financial relief to school districts in establishing school-based programs.

The School-age Parent Center was begun as a cooperative effort between William Beaumont Army Medical Center and the El Paso Independent School District. Initially, the school was located at William Beaumont Army Medical Center, but later was moved to an El Paso Independent School District facility.

The location of a special school is important. Very often the school becomes identified as the property of the entity supplying the space. However, in this instance, a plus in locating at the Army medical facility was the availability of physicians and nurses who assisted in health care instruction and staff training in the early days of program development. After the relocation to a new facility, this contact was for the most part lost, and it was necessary to secure other community contacts in the area of health care.

The format for instruction at SPC was designed to follow the regular school academic program. A young woman was able to continue her required studies as well as take classes in family life, labor and delivery, child development, health, family planning, modified physical education, and Lamaze training. Students enrolled in the program at any time in their pregnancy, and could stay until the end of the semester after the birth of the infant.

Comprehensive Services Offered

A comprehensive array of services was offered at SPC which helped to ensure that participants would use services available in the community. On-site child care was provided by the YWCA. On-site health services were offered through weekly health clinics coordinated by health care providers in the community. Counseling, social work services, and parenting training were available.

Most often the success of a program depends on the personal qualities of its staff. Relationships established between staff and participants were important, and served as the basis for all other services offered. Two critical elements of successful programming were present at SPC—a caring atmosphere and easily available services. The major missing component was the ability to provide long-term support.

A major goal was to help young people
make better use of community resources.

In 1983, the school district was approached by the El Paso Community Foundation to participate in a nationwide two-year demonstration research project known as Project Redirection. This project was funded partially by the Ford Foundation and partially by the El Paso Community Foundation and the City-County Health Department. This project was targeted to pregnant teens and young parents aged seventeen or younger who were from low-income families.

A major goal of the Ford Foundation project was to help these young people make better use of community resources by offering a wide range of services through a single program. The project objectives were to influence teens to complete school, to delay subsequent pregnancies, and to prepare for future employment. All objectives were aimed toward the ultimate goals of personal responsibility and economic self-sufficiency. Since these, essentially, were the goals of the SPC program, and since most services required by Project Redirection were in place at a single site, the meshing of the demonstration project and the school program was a natural.

The addition of Project Redirection did much to enhance the opportunities for self-sufficiency of the seventy SPC students who met eligibility requirements, and who participated in the project over the two-year period. The project served as a vehicle for long-term follow-up by incorporating the concept of volunteer community women to assist participants in understanding and attaining program goals. Peer support groups met weekly and did much to enhance the self-esteem and emotional growth of each participant. The addition of Project Redirection to SPC provided vocational information to all two hundred SPC students as well as specific vocational training to the seventy project enrollees.

Recruit School Dropouts

During the second year of the demonstration, consideration was given to expanding the size of the project by recruiting school dropouts. To achieve this, Project Redirection and staff formed an advisory group to explore methods of identifying and attracting teens who had left school. The advisory group was composed of interested community leaders and service providers and did much toward publicizing and lending credibility both to the SPC program and to the Project Redirection component.

The project was now providing long-term support, and was beginning to be seen as a community endeavor. The advisory group assisted in documenting the need for services for teen parents in the community. They helped secure funds to provide these services through the combined efforts of the YWCA, El Paso Community Foundation, City-County Health Department, Texas Tech Allied Health Services, Thomason Family Planning, and the El Paso Independent School District. These community agencies, whose representatives were members of the advisory group, gradually began to assume responsibility for pooling resources to work together.

In August, 1985, at the completion of the Ford Foundation Funding, the Advisory Council submitted a proposal to the Texas Department of Human Services requesting funds for a new expanded program. The goal was to provide comprehensive support to all pregnant and parenting teens in El Paso County regardless of income. The YWCA of El Paso was asked to become the administrative agency, and under its leadership, more than fifteen social service agencies and school districts pledged support in the effort to:

- identify pregnant or parenting teens and assist them in using existing community services.
- coordinate existing services for this population and develop new services where necessary.

The name **"Project Redirection"** was retained for the new county-wide effort.

Project Redirection is composed of several components, each of which is important to the overall success of the program. Each of these components has changed and developed over the past years to meet the needs of parenting teens more effectively.

Staffing and Case Management

Project Redirection staff consists of a program administrator who has responsibility for overall program management, an associate administrator/evaluator whose major duties include development and maintenance of a computerized tracking system, a project secretary, and six case managers. Each case manager has responsibility for an assigned caseload in one of the six designated areas that comprise El Paso County. A director of volunteer services supervises a large volunteer component of the program.

The level of need which a client has determines the extent of case manager involvement.

Case management is the most important direct service provided by Project Redirection. Because of an enrollment ranging from one thousand to twelve hundred, and a small number of case managers (six), a unique system has been devised to enable each case manager to maintain a caseload ranging from 150 to 250.

All case management services include an intake process whereby needs are assessed. An individual client plan is developed pinpointing areas requiring immediate action. A standard outline for assessment and a format for developing the client plan is used. Regularly scheduled area peer support meetings and a monthly newsletter mailed to all clients assist case managers in maintaining client contact.

The level of need which a client has determines the extent of case manager involvement. To ensure the effectiveness of the case management system, case loads are divided into five levels of activity with each client being assigned an appropriate level. Clients may shift frequently from one level to another as their needs and life circumstances change.

Clients falling into **Level I** include most new referrals and those requiring constant or weekly contact in order to implement the client plan.

Level II includes those clients requiring at least a monthly contact with the case manager in order to maintain the client plan.

Level III clients are generally doing well, most are receiving services, are in school or training, and require quarterly contacts to monitor progress.

Case managers complete periodic reports and updates on clients falling into Levels I, II, and III.

Prior to exiting from Project Redirection, clients may be placed in **Level IV** for a six-month period. During this time they receive the monthly newsletter and may attend peer support meetings. After a six-month period, the case manager will conduct an exit interview prior to termination from the project.

Level V clients are those who are not interested in the program at this time, but are assessed by the case manager as having a need for services. If a client remains at this level for three months, the case will be terminated from the case manager's active list, but will remain on the mailing list for newsletters and special mailings. No updates or reports are prepared on Levels IV and V clients.

A computerized monitoring system has been developed for the Levels System of case management. A periodic computer print-out for each case manager outlines client status and flags those due for personal contact. Clients are terminated from Project Redirection for a variety of reasons. If the case manager believes that the participant still needs services and might request re-entry into the program at a future date, the case may be assigned to Level V.

When Teresa, sixteen, came into the program, she was a belligerant chola complete with tatooed black tear drop. After two years of support, she has turned her life around. She earned a GED (Graduate Equivalency Diploma), went through Job Corps training, and is presently employed in a YWCA day care center. She is planning to enter community college to take child development courses in the hope of becoming a day care director one day. Her son is three.

In addition to making referrals to appropriate agencies, case managers are involved in teaching clients how to access and use available services effectively. The persistent personal contact, encouragement, and monitoring by the case manager is often the key to motivating teen parents to take charge of their own lives.

A spin-off benefit of the case management system has been assessing the appropriateness of existing community services. Many agencies have modified operating procedures to serve teen parents more effectively as a result of case manager input. Gaps in service have been identified, and the project itself has attempted to initiate programs which have, in some cases, been continued by an existing agency.

It is felt that the success of the Project Redirection service delivery and case management model is dependent on several key features:

Decentralized Staff. Case managers are out-stationed in the areas they serve, usually housed in a branch of the YWCA.

Individualized Case Plans. Redirection does not have a structured sequence of activities that all clients are expected to complete. Rather, each plan is based on needs of the teen, and modified as needs change or are met.

Use of Existing Public Services. To the extent possible, clients are referred to schools, health clinics, and other public agencies for services.

Variable Contact with Staff. Frequency of contact with staff varies depending on individual client's level of need.

Use of Volunteers. Case managers benefit from the assistance of volunteers assigned to those clients who need extra attention.

Education Services

The educational component of this project is directed toward keeping teen parents in school until graduation or, if appropriate, assisting them in securing a GED certificate with subsequent vocational training.

---

*Liaisons monitor attendance
and offer encouragement
through individual and group support sessions.*

Superintendents of nine county school districts were contacted individually and asked for assistance in referring teen parents to Project Redirection. In return, Project Redirection staff assisted school personnel in influencing teen parents to return to and remain in school.

School districts are often reluctant to work closely with community agencies, and such might have been the case here except for the credibility of the YWCA in the El Paso community. The Y was widely known for its successful program implementation and effective financial management. This fact, coupled with the school districts' desire to receive assistance in serving teen parents, greatly facilitated cooperation with the schools.

The two major school districts in the county were already providing alternative educational services to pregnant teens. The smaller rural districts were interested in bonding together to develop a cooperative educational facility.

Project Redirection has been highly successful in influencing teen parents to stay in school. To assist case managers in this effort, **Project Redirection School Liaisons** have been established in each of the high schools in the county. The School Liaison is usually a classroom teacher or a counselor selected by the school principal and paid a small stipend by Project Redirection. School Liaisons stay in close contact with case managers as well as with all teen parents in a specific high school. Liaisons monitor attendance and offer encouragement through individual and group support sessions.

A significant number of identified teens were older school dropouts and were not likely to return to high school. For these clients, Project Redirection and El Paso Community College (EPCC) developed a block of enrichment classes which offered GED and secretarial training as well as counseling and practical life skills information.

Initially this class was funded by Texas Department of Human Services, and the Office of Adolescent Pregnancy Programs (OAPP/DHHS) and administered through a contractual agreement with the college. Later the Community College contracted directly with Job Training Partnership Act (JTPA) for funding (using section 123 funds). Title IV funds are now available, and the Teen Parent Program has become a permanent instructional arrangement at EPCC.

Older dropout teens are also referred to Private Industry Council (PIC) which has cooperated with Project Redirection in selecting a specific intake specialist to work directly with program staff. The on-going support of the case managers has resulted in a significant number of participants being placed in PIC training programs.

Lilia, non-English speaking, joined the program two years ago. She has improved her English skills and her self-esteem ten-fold. She secured her GED through our Community College class last summer where she also improved her typing and computer skills. She is now in advanced training through PIC to build on her secretarial skills. We feel her future is assured. Her daughter is two, and Lilia hasn't been pregnant again.

Additional education opportunities for dropouts were developed with the assistance of Region XIX Educational Service Center, which received a grant from Texas Education Agency

(TEA). to provide a GED/Vocational Training program for single parents in three rural school districts. This program has been successful for a small number of students, and offers a much needed referral source in an isolated rural area.

The identification of several sub-groups of teen parents having divergent needs has led to the development of these innovative approaches. Staff has realized the program environment frequently must be changed to accommodate varying educational needs of this population.

Health Care Coordinated

Initially the major health care providers in the El Paso community were approached and asked how they, by working together, could provide inexpensive and readily accessible health care to teen parents and their children.

After the initial hurdle of overcoming turfdom, and the reality that there would be no health care funds available from the program grant, the health care providers devised a plan of shared responsibility.

Health care providers became a major source of referral to Project Redirection through the referral system devised by program staff. Representatives from the schools and the health care agencies were members of the Project Redirection Advisory Council, and were given positive feedback on how their referrals were handled.

In 1986, using a $10,000 grant from El Paso Community Foundation, Project Redirection developed contracts with health care agencies to provide clinic care at each of the two alternative school sites in the county. Texas Tech School of Medicine provided staff to administer prenatal care on site, and City-County Health Department loaned equipment and provided well-baby services to each alternative school site.

In 1987, due to decreased staff and funding, Texas Tech discontinued on-site prenatal care. However, the El Paso Independent School District, in order to ensure school attendance on clinic days, provided bus transportation for those students from the El Paso Independent School District. The health department continued on-site well-baby care until the end of the 1987 school year when it was determined that the majority of young mothers were using neighborhood clinics.

Health care needs of participants are presently being served by referrals to existing agencies. The majority of referrals are made to Texas Tech Adolescent Clinic at R. E. Thomason General Hospital, and the thirteen City-County Health Department neighborhood clinics. All eligible participants are referred to the Women, Infants and Children (WIC) food program.

Project Redirection staff cooperates with the Adolescent Clinic by providing weekly educational workshops to teens waiting to be examined. In exchange, processing for Project Redirection has become a part of the clinic intake procedure. Close contact is maintained with City-County Health Department staff through occasional joint meetings to share ideologies and refine referral procedures.

Program participants are referred to Planned Parenthood and to the R. E. Thomason Family Planning Clinic for family planning counseling and supplies.

Close contact and cooperation between health care agencies and Project Redirection staff does much to ensure that each participant receives adequate and continuing health services.

Use of Volunteers

An important part of the Project Redirection support system has been the use of volunteers to assist case managers in providing support and guidance to clients needing extra attention. The project presently maintains a corps of approximately 150 volunteers.

Early in the program implementation, it became apparent that increasing case load size left little time for case managers to recruit volunteers. To ease this situation, a grant was received from the Office of Voluntarism, Department of Health and Human Services. This enabled the project to employ three volunteer coordinators who then assumed responsibility for recruitment and training of volunteers.

Volunteers act as role models, often provide transportation, or may be responsible for tutoring, clerical tasks, and telephoning. An intake/screening process assists in the selection of volunteers. These procedures adhere closely to policies already established by the YWCA Board of Directors.

Each volunteer is required to attend training sessions provided by Project Redirection staff to prepare them to deal with teen parents. Topics covered include decision making, goal setting, communication skills, community agency referrals, parenting, and family planning. When trained, volunteers are assigned to one or more teens. The volunteer works under the supervision of a volunteer coordinator, and receives ongoing support and training.

Day Care Homes Augment School Centers

The major force behind the success of Project Redirection in keeping teen parents in school has been the provision of day care. Many clients are unable to participate in education and training programs unless child care is available. Project Redirection maintains two day care centers in public school settings and contracts with registered day care homes in order to meet the increasing need for day care.

The two centers maintained by Project Redirection are located in the alternative schools for pregnant students, and are staffed and equipped by the YWCA. The school systems provide utilities, janitorial services, and space, which must meet state guidelines. These centers are operated under the same standards as other YWCA day care facilities.

Since the young mothers are in the same building with their infants, they may spend the lunch hour with their babies. Breastfed infants are brought to their mothers in class so that classroom instruction is not interrupted.

A Project Redirection day care coordinator, under the supervision of the YWCA Day Care Executive, is responsible for locating and evaluating day care homes, placing children, and monitoring placements. Day care homes are registered by the State of Texas and must comply with all state guidelines. Caregivers receive periodic training and must be certified in food handling, CPR, and first aid.

Day care homes have been located close to each high school in the county to facilitate teens' use of services. Some have developed into a support system for young mothers with the caregiver becoming a role model and mentor. Both school-based centers and day care homes offer excellent opportunities for instruction in parenting and child care techniques.

In order to receive day care services, a young mother must be referred by her case manager, and she must be participating regularly in a school or training program. At the time of application for day care, the teen is informed of the weekly cost which the program pays for the care of her infant. A small fee is assessed based on the teen's rather than the family income. Fees are often waived or lowered depending upon circumstances. The major benefit in assessing fees is to help clients recognize and plan for the costs of child care as they strive for self-sufficiency.

Carole and Karen, seventeen, participated in the Project Redirection PIC-funded summer program and received their GEDs in two months. The twins applied for further PIC training, and PIC has agreed to fund both young mothers at International Business College. Project Redirection is providing day care for their babies, and volunteer and case manager support to Carole and Karen.

Emergency Housing Available

In the early days of the program, emergency housing was provided on a limited basis through a contractual arrangement with a private facility. Lack of adequate supervision prompted a sub-committee of the Advisory Council to develop a foster home program with Lee Moor Children's Home to ensure supervised placement for the young mother and her baby. Lee Moor Children's Home is a foster home licensing agency, and in accordance with a contractual agreement, is responsible for the licensing and supervision of the foster homes used by Project Redirection participants.

Foster home placement is made only in cases of dire need, and is usually short-term. Each placement is carefully monitored and formally reviewed on a month-to-month basis.

Before placement can occur, a conference is held with the teen, her parent or guardian if possible, the case manager, foster parent, and representative from the Lee Moor Home. A thorough processing procedure is completed which complies with the Texas Department of Human Services (TDHS) minimum standards for foster home placement. A written agreement between the agency and the teen's legal parent or conservator is signed, and a service plan is developed outlining the responsibilities of both teens and their parents.

The case manager is responsible for weekly contact with the teen, and an evaluation conference is held within thirty days of placement. During the placement period, all parties concerned work toward a stable and permanent housing arrangement for the teen and her infant. Costs for the placement are assumed by Project Redirection assisted by those parents who are financially able to contribute.

Transportation System Inadequate

Transportation in El Paso County is a great barrier to providing services to teens. The city bus system is cumbersome with few direct routes. Public transportation in the rural areas of the county is non-existent.

A limited number of student bus tickets are provided by the Project to enable clients to get to school, day care, or training programs. Volunteers often provide transportation to and from clinic appointments and peer support meetings. On occasion, case managers provide emergency transportation.

Therapeutic Counseling Provided

For clients needing such services, therapeutic counseling is provided by referral to appropriate agencies. A licensed psychologist, serving as a volunteer, assists with psychological evaluations and counseling.

Informal counseling is provided by the case managers, and has been a motivating force in helping clients take advantage of opportunities available to them.

To strengthen counseling contacts, a monthly newsletter is sent to each client. This has proved to be an effective outreach tool in keeping clients informed of activities, as well as involving inactive teens.

The use of peer support groups has proved to be successful in providing instruction and esteem building activities. Each case manager meets with teens in her area a minimum of once a month.

Frequently, guest speakers are used to provide information on such topics as family planning, household management, career exploration, child and spousal abuse, human sexuality, parenting, and other topics. To the extent possible, teens are involved in the planning and management of these groups.

Teen Father Involvement

To provide information and support to teen fathers, a couples program was developed during the summer of 1987. Forty couples meeting in various areas of the county were enrolled to explore communication, values, decision making, family planning, and financial management.

Separate funding was available for this program. This enabled the project to secure the services of two male counselors who worked under the supervision of Project Redirection staff in developing a specific curriculum for use with teen couples. The information gathered from the couples class has proved valuable in providing peer support groups for young fathers, and in recruiting male volunteers and mentors.

Project Redirection is in the process of developing a teen fathers component to include services comparable to those being offered to young mothers.

Family Center

A proposal was submitted to the Department of Health and Human Services and funds secured to establish a family center known as El Nido de la Familia (The Family Nest). This center is located in a YWCA branch in a predominantly Hispanic neighborhood, and serves young couples involved in a first pregnancy.

The philosophy of El Nido is based on early intervention. Goals are to strengthen the young male's perception of his role as a father, and to support the involvement of the extended families of the young couples.

The major goals are to strengthen parenting abilities, enhance the functioning of the family unit, and promote responsibility and self-sufficiency. A specific, culturally-sensitive curriculum has been developed. This includes activities emphasizing shared participation of male and female in food preparation, formula and infant food preparation, prenatal care, child care, budgeting and wise shopping procedures, nutrition, self-awareness, and Lamaze training.

A specific unit on parenting skills includes such topics as discipline, toilet-training, responsibility and personal coping skills, safety in the household, and involvement of the extended family.

A young couple makes a commitment to attend weekly training sessions for a period of six months. The teen father and the extended family units are encouraged to participate in the care of and responsibility for the infant.

A longitudinal study on child abuse and recurrence, involving El Nido participants, is being conducted under the direction of Dr. Stephen Bablock of the University of Utah Health Department. Early findings are positive.

It is hoped that a by-product of the El Nido program will be the prevention of pregnancy in siblings of participants through the education and involvement of extended family units.

Prevention Component

Late in the second project year, Redirection received funding from the Junior League of El Paso and the National YWCA Board of Directors to implement a nationally tested pregnancy prevention model called Peer Approach Counseling by Teens, known as PACT. A PACT Coordinator was hired who contacted a large school district in the county and secured their cooperation.

Through counselors in the schools, a corps of teens was identified to be trained as PACT teens. During the summer months, these teens received 120 hours of intensive instruction in the areas of human sexuality, communication skills, decision making, and public speaking.

During the school year, PACT-trained teens assisted school counselors in teaching other unresponsive peers, gave presentations on human sexuality in classrooms, and addressed civic groups throughout the city.

Other school districts have expressed interest in the Peer Counseling Program.

The number of teens to be trained during the ensuing year has increased significantly. Low income teens who meet PIC requirements are selected using YWCA summer employment allotments, and are paid by PIC for their participation in the PACT training.

The goals and underlying philosophy of the El Paso Project Redirection program have remained stable since its inception. However, components have been added and operational techniques modified and refined during the past year.

It is expected that this process of modification will continue with input being received through the case managers and the Advisory Council.

The Advisory Council is a working council which explores program needs and makes recommendations for change. All major policy change in program operation originates with the Advisory Council with final approval being given by the YWCA Board of Directors. In this sense, Project Redirection is truly a community-based program operated by and for the community of El Paso County.

Success Stories

For the young women and young men in Project Redirection, success is measured in small increments. For them, success can be passing a history class, learning to cope with a colicky baby, or getting a job for the first time. And each success is a cause for celebration.

One pregnant fifteen-year-old was referred to Project Redirection when her parents kicked her out of the house and, subsequently, moved out of town. Having nowhere else to turn, she moved in with her boyfriend's family in another school district. Because she didn't know the whereabouts of her family and had no legal guardian, the school refused to enroll her—

until a project case manager intervened. Now sixteen, she is on the honor roll.

Another pregnant fifteen-year-old was in a bad home situation when she began participating in the project. She wanted to move in with her boyfriend's family, but a volunteer worked with both teenagers and helped them reconcile with their families. Now seventeen years old, the two are back in school and working. The teen mother is living with her family.

A high school student contacted Project Redirection when she thought she might be pregnant. A case manager arranged a pregnancy test for her and helped her break the news to her parents when the results were positive. The girl dropped out of school, enrolled in a GED program, successfully completed her GED, and enrolled in business college where she also completed her studies. She is now employed full time, and supports herself and her child. She is seventeen.

Each day brings a new story as pregnant teens and teenage mothers and fathers strive to improve their lives and the lives of their children. Project Redirection is working—for all of us.

APPENDIX

Barbara Huberman
NC Coalition on Adol. Pregnancy
1300 Baxter, #171
Charlotte, NC 28204
704/335-1313

Sr. Maureen Joyce
Community Maternity Services
27 N. Main
Albany, NY 12203
518/482-8836

The Hon. Linda Larason
OK State Rep., District 88
931 N.W. 15th
Oklahoma City, OK 73106
405/521-2711

Myra Nash-Johnson
Catholic Charities
721 N. LaSalle
Chicago, IL 60610
312/266-6100, x 299

Ellen Peach, R.N., F.N.P.
28 Averill Terrace
Waterville, ME 04901
207/877-6969

Judy Peterson
BETA
4680 Underhill Road
Orlando, FL 32807
407/277-1942

Mary Polk
TDHS—Ass't. to Commissioner
P.O. Box 2960 (000-W)
Austin, TX 78769
512/450-3037

David Reese
Southwest District Health Dept.
920 Main
Caldwell, ID 83605
208/459-0744

Karen Schrock
MI Dept. of Health
P.O. Box 30195
Lansing, MI 48909
517/335-8885

Ann M. Wilson, ACSW
NJ Network on Adol. Pregnancy
73 Easton Avenue
New Brunswick, NJ 08903
201/932-8636

John Winn
FL Dept. of Education
1701 Capitol
Tallahassee, FL 32399
904/488-1611

VOLUNTEER CONSULTANTS

Mary Olmstead Butcher
3661 Ludgate Road
Shaker Heights, OH 44120
216/991-7974

Caroline Gaston
New Futures
5400 Cutler, NE
Albuquerque, NM 87110
505/883-5680

Lois Gatchell
5208 S. Atlanta Avenue
Tulsa, OK 74105
918/743-2915

Anita Gallegos
March of Dimes
502 South Verdugo Drive
Burbank, CA 91502
818/972-9449

NOAPP Network EDITOR
Jeanne Lindsay
Morning Glory Press
6595 San Haroldo Way
Buena Park, CA 90620
714/828-1998

NOAPP OFFICE
Sharon Rodine, M.Ed.
NOAPP
P.O. Box 2365
Reston, VA 22090
703/435-3948

Resource Programs and People

Following is a list of the people and programs included in *Teen Pregnancy Challenge, Book One: Strategies for Change.* These resources are arranged alphabetically by *program* name followed by the name of the quoted individual.

These are the people we especially want to thank for their wonderful help in the research for this book. We have each talked with most of them.

Sharon Rodine, as Executive Director of NOAPP, is in constant contact with adolescent pregnancy prevention and care program providers throughout the United States. Jeanne Lindsay had a delightful time interviewing about ninety of these caring people in preparation for *Teen Pregnancy Challenge.* Those who are quoted in *Book Two* are listed in that book's Appendix.

The enthusiasm of these individuals, who care so much about young people, and who are making a difference in the lives of many, is inspiring and contagious. You may want to contact some of them.

Adolescent Family Education, Tucson Unified School District
Sherry Betts, Director
1010 East Tenth Street
Tucson, AZ 85717
602/798-2774

Adolescent Health Service/MCV
Richard Brookman, M.D.
Box 151
Medical College of Virginia
Richmond, VA 23298-0151
804/786-9408

Adolescent Pregnancy Child Watch, Los Angeles County
Jan Kern, President
315 West Ninth
Los Angeles, CA 90015
213/689-0090

Adolescent Pregnancy Coalition
Margaret Clark
74 Winthrop Street
Augusta, ME 04330
207/622-5188

Adolescent Single Parent Program, Bowie High School
Agnes Kuhn, Teacher
12500 Annapolis Road
Bowie, MD 20715
301/464-8500

Arizona Family Planning Council
Kate Hanley, Community Relations Director
2920 N. 24th Avenue—#26
Phoenix, AZ 85015
602/258-5777

Arts of Living Institute, Catholic Charities
Myra Nash Johnson, Director
721 North LaSalle
Chicago, IL 60610
312/266-6100, x 299

BETA
Judy Peterson, Director
4680 Underhill Road
Orlando, FL 32807
407/277-1942

Boulder Valley Schools Teen Parenting Program
Gloria Parmerlee-Greiner, Director
1515 Greenbriar Boulevard
Boulder, CO 80303
303/494-1006

Center for Research on Women
Fern Marx
Wellesley College
Wellesley, MA 02181
617/235-0320

Cities in Schools, Inc.
Bill Milliken
1023 15th Street, NW, Suite 600
Washington, DC 20005
202/861-0230

Coalition on Responsible Parenting and Adolescent Sexuality
(CORPAS)
Jesse Sandoval, Senior Consultant
Youth Planning Commission
Community Council of Greater Dallas
2121 Main Street, Suite 500
Dallas, TX 75201-4321
214/741-5851

CONNECT, A Program for Pregnant and Parenting Teens
Ann Sandven, Project Director
Terry Reilly Health Services
1515 Third Street North
Nampa, ID 83651
208/467-4431

The Door—A Center of Alternatives
Michaele P. White, Aministrator
121 Sixth Avenue
New York, NY 10013
212/941-9090

Fairbanks Health Center
Mary E. O'Bryan
800 Airport Way
Fairbanks, AK 99701
907/452-1801

Family Focus—Lawndale
Gilda Ferguson-Smith, Director
3600 West Ogden Avenue
Chicago, IL 60623
312/521-3306

Family Resource Coalition
230 North Michigan Avenue, Suite 1625
Chicago, IL 60601
312/726-4750

Family TALKS
Ellen Peach
28 Averill Terrace
Waterville, ME 04901
207/877-6969

Horizon Youth Services Center
Margo Jaenike, Executive Director
806 Morgan Boulevard, Suite K
Harlingen, TX 78550
512/428-1453

The HUB
Mary Morales, Director/Clinic Administrator
Planned Parenthood
349 East 149th Street
Bronx, NY 10451
212/292-8000

International Newspaper Advertising and Marketing Executives Foun.
Susan Schoebel, Foundation Director
11600 Sunrise Valley Drive
Reston, VA 22091
703/648-1168

Lady Pitts School
Peggy A. Clapp, Principal
820 E. Knapp—Third Floor
Milwaukee, WI 53202
414/278-0406

Larason, Linda
Oklahoma State Representative, District 88
931 N.W. 15th
Oklahoma City, OK 73106
405/521-2711

Maine Young Fathers Project
Sally Brown, Director
Human Services Resource Development Institute
University of Southern Maine
96 Falmouth Street
Portland, ME 04103
207/780-4216

Male Youth Project, Shiloh Baptist Church
Andre Watson, Director
1510 Ninth Street, N.W.
Washington, DC 20001
202/232-4200

March of Dimes Birth Defects Foundation
Mary Hughes, National Vice President for Community Services
1275 Mamaroneck Avenue
White Plains, NY 10605
914/428-7100

March of Dimes Birth Defects Foundation—National Capital Area
1700 South Quincy Street, Suite 220
Arlington, VA 22206
703/824-0111

Margaret Hudson Program
Nancy Pate, Executive Director
P.O. Drawer 6340
Tulsa, OK 74114
918/585-8163

Maternal Health Center
Tom Fedje, Director
852 Middle Road, Box 11369
Bettendorf, IA 52722
319/359-6633

McBride, Dennis, Research Consultant
2309 Cincinnati Street
Steilacoom, WA 98388
206/582-1506

Mecklenburg Council on Adolescent Pregnancy
Barbara Ziegler, Director
1300 Baxter Street, Suite 170
Charlotte, NC 28204
704/332-6721

Medina Children's Services
June Beleford
123 16th Avenue
P.O. Box 22638
Seattle, WA 98122
206/324-9470

Mentor Mother Program—Cooperative Extension Service
Jane Hildenbrand, Director
9245 North Meridian Street, Suite 118
Indianapolis, IN 46260
317/253-0871

Michigan Department of Public Health
Karen Schrock, Chief of the Eastern Regional Division
P.O. Box 30195
Lansing, MI 48909
517/335-8885

Mott, Charles Stewart, Foundation
Marilyn Steele
Mott Foundation Building
Flint, MI 48502-1851
313/238-5651

New Futures School
Caroline Gaston, Principal
5400 Cutler, N.E.
Albuquerque, NM 87100
505/883-5680

New Horizons Program
Mary Foster
101 North Briaroaks Road
Burleson, TX 76028
817/295-6761

New Jersey Network for Family Life Education
Susan Wilson
Building 4087, Kilmer Campus
Rutgers University
New Brunswick, NJ 08903
201/932-7929

North Carolina Coalition on Adolescent Pregnancy
Barbara Huberman, Executive Director
1300 Baxter, #171
Charlotte, NC 28204
704/335-1313

Northwest Area Foundation
West 975 First National Bank Building
St. Paul, MN 55101 1373
612/2240-9635

Ounce of Prevention Fund
Laura Devon Jones, Director, Media Relations
188 West Randolph, Suite 2200
Chicago, IL 60601
312/853-6080

Our Place/Family Focus
Delores Holmes, Director
2010 Dewey
Evanston, IL 60201
312/475-7570

Philliber Research Associates
Philliber, Susan
145 Lucas Avenue
Accord, NY 12404
914/687-7175

Polk, Mary, Assistant to the Commissioner
Texas Department of Human Services
P.O. Box 2960 (000-W)
Austin, TX 78769
512/450-3037

Postponing Sexual Involvement Program
Marie E. Mitchell
Teen Services Program—Grady Memorial Hospital
80 Butler Street, S.E.
Atlanta, GA 30335
404/222-2302

Private Industry Council (PIC) of Lehigh Valley, Inc.
1601 Union Boulevard
P.O. Box 2287
Allentown, PA 18001-2287
215/437-5627

Project PIECES
Susan McGee
Newton-Conover Middle School
Newton, NC 28658
704/465-0122

School Age Mothers/Infant Development (SAPID)
Ronda Simpson, Teen Parent Coordinator Consultant
Department of Alternative Education
560 J Street, Suite 290
Sacramento, CA 95814
916/327-2161

School-Based Clinic Support Center
Sharon Lovick, Director
5650 Kirby Drive, #203
Houston, TX 77005
713/664-7400

Sisterhood of Black Single Mothers
Daphne Busby
1360 Fulton Street, Suite 423
Brooklyn, NY 11216

Southwest District Health Department
David Recse, Director
920 Main
Caldwell, ID 83605
208/459-0744

Student-Parent Center
Kathleen Fojtik
920 Miller
Ann Arbor, MI 48103
313/994-2018

Teen Mother Program
Pat Alviso
ABC Unified School District
12222 Cuesta
Cerritos, CA 90701
213/926-5566 x 2423

Teen Parent Program
3377 North Boulevard
Baton Rouge, LA 70806
504/342-6029

Teen Renaissance
Sue Dolezal, Teacher
607 South Joplin Street
Aurora, CO 80017
303/659-4830

Teen Talk
Patricia Minter
Forsythe County Health Department
P.O. Box 2975
Winston-Salem, NC 27102
919/727-2890

Teenage Parent Program
Georgia Chaffee, Principal
Jefferson County Schools
1100 Sylvia
Louisville, KY 40217
502/473-8245

TEXNET
Karen Quebe, Director
300 East Huntland Drive, Suite 122
Austin, TX 78752
512/444-8648

Urban Middle Schools Adolescent Pregnancy Prevention
Michele A. Cahill, School and Community Services
Academy for Educational Development
100 Fifth Avenue
New York, NY 10011
212/243-1110

Young Families Program
Marge Eliason
2911 Beech Avenue
Billings, MT 59102
406/245-7328

Youth Health Services
Fran Jackson, Director
971 Harrison Avenue
Elkins, WV 26241
304/636-9450

YWCA of Fort Worth and Tarrant County
512 West Fourth Street
Ft. Worth, TX 76102
817/332-6191

Resource Organizations

The following organizations are concerned about the teen pregnancy challenge, and some may have affiliates in your community or region. You may want to contact some of them for assistance as you work to meet the teen pregnancy challenge in your community.

Alan Guttmacher Institute
2010 Massachusetts Avenue, N.W.
Washington, DC 20036
202/296-4012
*Non-profit research, policy analysis and public education organization. Publishes **Family Planning Perspectives** and the **Washington Memo.***

American Association of University Women
2401 Virginia Avenue, N.W.
Washington, DC 20037
202/785-7753

*Developed a briefing paper on adolescent pregnancy; some
local affiliates are interested in adolescent pregnancy projects.*

American College of Obstetricians and Gynecologists
409 Twelfth Street, S.W.
Washington, DC 20024
202/638-5577
*Resources include media programs as well as research, publica-
tions, and information especially for health care professionals.
Contact them concerning annually updated **Public Service
Television Announcements** designed to reduce unintended teen
pregnancy. Includes public service television announcements in
English and Spanish.*

American Home Economics Association
1555 King Street
Alexandria, VA 22314
703/706-4600
*Special projects, task forces, and resources on adolescent
pregnancy for home economists and others.*

American Red Cross—Emergency and Community Services
17th and E Street, N.W.
Washington, DC 20006
202/639-3016
*"RAP—Reaching Adolescents and Parents," a parent-child
communication program which targets fifth through seventh
graders. Discusses self-esteem, values, media influence, puberty,
goals, decision-making; deals indirectly with adolescent
pregnancy.*

ASPO/Lamaze
1840 Wilson Boulevard, Suite 204
Arlington, VA 22201
703/524-7802
*Promotes Lamaze method of childbirth and prepared parent-
hood.*

Association of Junior Leagues
660 First Street
New York, NY 10016-3241
212/683-1515
Provides **Teen Outreach Program.** *Some local chapters of the Junior League provide funding for adolescent pregnancy prevention and parenting projects.*

Big Brothers/Big Sisters
230 North Thirteenth Street
Philadelphia, PA 19107
215/567-2748
Youth-serving agency with affiliates throughout the country. Links adult community volunteers with young people in need of a mentor and friend.

Boys Clubs of America
771 First Avenue
New York, NY 10017
212/557-5511
Stand Up and Be Counted! *is a national program to prevent alcohol use, drug use, and pregnancy among young people.*

Center for Population Options
1012 Fourteenth Street, N.W., Suite 1200
Washington, DC 20005
202/347-5700
Programs and information related to adolescent pregnancy prevention. School-Based Clinic Support Center under the auspices of CPO.

Child Welfare League of America
440 First Street, N.W.
Washington, DC 20001
202/638-2952
Advocacy organization working on a variety of child welfare issues. Includes Crittenton centers.

Children's Defense Fund
122 C Street, N.W.
Washington, DC 20001
202/628-8787
Advocacy organization focused on the needs of children; adolescent pregnancy and parenting data and publications.

Extension Service/USDA
U.S. Department of Agriculture
Home Economics and Human Nutrition
Washington, DC 20250
202/879-7590
Includes both the Family Life programming and the 4-H/Youth programming. (See National 4-H Council.)

Family Resource Coalition
230 North Michigan Avenue, Suite 1625
Chicago, IL 60601
312/726-4750
Membership network for programs interested in family and parenting issues/resources.

Family Support Administration (FSA/DHHS)
Department of Health and Human Services
370 L'Enfant Promenade S.W.
Washington, DC 20447
202/760-8113
Lead agency for Secretary's Teen Pregnancy Prevention Panel.

Future Homemakers of America
1910 Association Drive
Reston, VA 22091
703/476-4900
Families in the Future, a cooperative peer education project of FHA and the March of Dimes Birth Defects Foundation, is designed to provide facts for future adults and potential parents that help them make informed, responsible decisions about individual and family health.

Girls Clubs of America
205 Lexington Avenue
New York, NY 10016
212/689-3700
Adolescent Pregnancy Program with four parts: 1) parent-child communication on sexuality, 2) postponing sexual involvement, 3) developing career aspirations, and 4) knowing and using health resources. Choices (girls) and Challenges (boys) curricula focus on career aspiration development.

Healthy Mothers, Healthy Babies Coalition
409 Twelfth Street, S.W.
Washington, DC 20024-2588
202/638-5577
A coalition of eighty-plus national voluntary, health profes-sional, and government agencies committed to improving maternal and infant health through education; includes adolescent pregnancy task force.

Joseph P. Kennedy, Jr., Foundation
1350 New York Avenue, N.W., Suite 500
Washington, DC 20005-4709
202/393-1250
Developed the Community of Caring curriculum. Some funding available for Community of Caring implementation.

National Center for Education in Maternal and Child Health
NCEMCH
R and 38th Street N.E.
Washington, DC 20057
202/625-8400
The Center is a link between the sources of information/services and the professionals in areas of maternal and child health; free materials.

National Committee on Adoption
2025 M Street, N.W., #512
Washington, DC 20036
202/328-8072
Adoption advocacy organization.

National Board YWCA of the USA
726 Broadway
New York, NY 10003
212/614-2700
A variety of teen pregnancy/parenting programs are being
implemented at YWCAs throughout the United States. National
office has several programs including video materials and a
peer education curriculum, PACT.

National Center for Child Abuse and Neglect (NCCAN)
Office of Human Development Services (OHDS/DHHS)
330 C Street S.W.
Washington, DC 20201
202/245-0586
National clearing house for information related to child abuse
and neglect issues.

National Center for Neighborhood Enterprise
1367 Connecticut Avenue, N.W.
Washington, DC 20036
202/331-1103
A research demonstration and development organization that
works with communities to develop successful enterprises
dealing with economic and social problems.

National Commission to Prevent Infant Mortality
330 C Street, S.W.
Washington, DC 20201
202/472-1364
Research and information about infant mortality.

National Council of Jewish Women
15 East 26th Street
New York, NY 10010
NCJW has a Center for the Child Research Institute which has
data and information on a wide variety of related topics.

National Family Planning and Reproductive Health Association
122 C Street, N.W., #380
Washington, DC 20001
202/628-3535
National network for family planning and reproductive health care providers.

National Forum for Black Public Administrators
1301 Pennsylvania Avenue, N.W., Suite 801
Washington, DC 20004
202/626-4906
Directs an adolescent pregnancy reduction project that includes data bank of programs.

National Governors Association
444 North Capitol Street, N.W.
Washington, DC 20001
202/624-5300
Had special task force on teen pregnancy during 1986-87; planning follow-up activities to support the development of state plans.

National Institute for Adolescent Pregnancy and Family Services
Center for Research in Human Development and Education
Temple University
Room 409-410 Seltzer Hall
1700 North Broad Street
Philadelphia, PA 19121
215/787-6208
Research, training and education information related to adolescent pregnancy and parenting.

National March of Dimes Birth Defects Foundation
1275 Mamaroneck Avenue
White Plains, NY 10605
914/428-7100

Provides educational materials, programs and funding related to encouraging good prenatal care and parenting.

National Mental Health Association
1021 Prince Street
Alexandria, VA 22314-2971
703/684-7722
Established an Office of Prevention which includes children and adolescents as target groups to be served.

National Organization on Adolescent Pregnancy and Parenting (NOAPP)
P.O. Box 2365
Reston, VA 22090
703/435-3948
National membership-based resource network for individuals and organizations interested in adolescent pregnancy, parenting and prevention issues and programs.

National 4-H Council
USDA/Extension Service
South Building—Room 3860
Washington, DC 20250
202/447-5332
Some state and local 4-H programs have initiated innovative programs dealing with parent-child communication, teen coping skills, and mentoring activities with teen mothers. Contact your state or county 4-H/Extension Service program for information on programs in your area.

National Urban League
500 East 62nd Street
New York, NY 10021
212/310-9000
Adolescent Male Responsibility Project, *a national public awareness campaign to encourage responsible male involvement in parenting and to highlight the male role in preventing adolescent pregnancies; sponsor wide variety of adolescent pregnancy prevention and care programs.*

Office of Adolescent Pregnancy Programs (OAPP)
Room 733-E, HHH Building
200 Independence Avenue, S.W.
Washington, DC 20201
202/245-7473
DHHS agency which funds and supervises federal programs related to adolescent pregnancy and parenting. Current funds target Adolescent Family Life programming.

Planned Parenthood Federation of America
810 Seventh Avenue
New York, NY 10019
212/541-7800
Offer a wide variety of education and service programs focused on the primary mission of prevention of unintended pregnancies for women of all ages. Promote "National Family Sexuality Education Month" each October, with ideas for local community activities.

School-Based Clinics Support Center
Sharon Lovick, Director
5650 Kirby Drive, Suite 203
Houston, TX 77005
703/664-7400

Sex Information and Education Council of the U.S. (SIECUS)
80 Fifth Avenue, #801
New York, NY 10011
212/929-2300
Resource and clearinghouse for sex information and education; advocate for healthy sexuality.

SHARE Resource Center
P.O. Box 30666
Bethesda, MD 20814
301/907-6523; 1-800-537-3788
Clearinghouse for adolescent pregnancy related materials; funded by the Family Support Administration (FSA/DHHS).

MANAGING THE MEDIA
A Fifteen-Step Plan

By Howard Klink, Public Affairs Director, Multnomah County
Department of Human Services, Portland, Oregon
Reprinted with permission from *Clinic News,* Winter, 1989

1. Designate a person who will be perceived as a **facilitator and an objective information source** to coordinate media activities.

2. Establish **policies and procedures** that ensure all media contacts will be coordinated through one person.

3. Develop a list of **beat or special assignment reporters** who are consistently assigned to your program's issues and maintain regular contact with them.

4. Identify potential **editorial support** in print and electronic media and initiate a regular flow of information to the appropriate person(s).

5. Identify **television and radio stations involved in public affairs programming.** Keep in regular contact with producers concerning topic suggestions, information resources, and local contacts.

6. Develop a list of **on-call media spokespeople,** including representatives from the clergy, parent groups, health professionals, and minority communities.

7. Prepare **short briefing papers** that are audience-specific and are free of human services jargon.

8. Make sure that **everyone likely to be contacted by the media has the same background information** and is communicating the same concise, limited number of messages.

9. **Conduct a forum** on your issues for news editors, reporters, and public affairs program producers.

10. **Invite friendly reporters** to assist in media training of agency spokespeople, community leaders, and your staff.

11. **Anticipate events likely to attract media attention** and adequately brief elected officials, school administrators, community leaders, and line staff.

12. **Structure, do not limit, media access** to agency and program staff or program sites.

13. **Don't give reporters "scoops."** Release information to everyone at the same time.

14. **Effectively use public opinion surveys** to focus your messages and document community support.

15. **Celebrate your successes publicly** through effective use of media events and press conferences.

Annotated Bibliography

Following is a selected bibliography of books and other resources dealing with adolescent pregnancy prevention and care program development issues. Additional resources are included in the Bibliography in *Teen Pregnancy Challenge, Book Two: Programs for Kids*.

We feel the following titles are especially relevant to the program development topics discussed in *Teen Pregnancy Challenge, Book One: Strategies for Change*.

Resources listed in the Bibliography in *Book 2: Programs for Kids* fit more readily on a specific spot on the adolescent pregnancy prevention continuum. That is, they deal more specifically with prevention of too-early pregnancy, prenatal care issues, and/or services for parenting teens and their children. There is almost no duplication in the two bibliographies. Some resources, however, are appropriate for both, and you may want to check the entries in both books.

Prices, when given, are from the 1988-1989 edition of *Books in Print*, or, when not listed in that publication, were obtained directly from the publisher. If you order a book directly from the publisher, check first with your public library or a bookstore to learn current prices. Then add $2.00 for shipping.

"75 Each Day" The Facts: Adolescent Pregnancy in North Carolina in 1989. 1989. The North Carolina Coalition on Adolescent Pregnancy. 1300 Baxter Street, Charlotte, NC 28204. 704/335-1313. 50 pp. $3.00.
Wonderful example of sharing facts about teenage pregnancy in a specific area. Packed with statistics, charts, trend descriptions, and other information.

AAUW. *"Coping with Teen Pregnancy: Community Strategies."* 1988. Publications, American Association of University Women, 2401 Virginia Avenue, N.W., Washington, DC 20037; 202/785-7753. 8 pp. $2.00. Bulk discount.
Issue brief which presents an overview of the teen pregnancy problem in the United States, ideas for community action strategies, and a list of resource groups and materials.

"Adolescent Sexuality Special Subject Bibliography January—December 1988." 1989. Planned Parenthood Federation of America, Inc., 810 Seventh Avenue, New York, NY 10019. 28 pp, $3.25.
This special subject bibliography is based on entries which have appeared in the 1988 issues of Current Literature in Family Planning, the Katharine Dexter McCormick Library's annotated bibliography of recent books, journal articles, and reports in the fields of family planning, sexuality education, and reproductive health.

Alternatives: The Report of the New Jersey Task Force on Adolescent Pregnancy. 1988. New Jersey Dept. of Health, Division of Community Health Services, 363 West State Street, CN 364, Trenton, NJ 08625. 609/292-8104. 64 pp.
Excellent report on services to pregnant adolescents, teen parents and those at risk in New Jersey.

Beyond Stereotypes: Who Becomes a Single Teenage Mother? 1988. The RAND Corporation, 1700 Main Street, P.O. Box 2138, Santa Monica, CA 90406-2138. 213/393-0411. 88 pp. $7.50.
Monograph contains good research information.

Brindis, Claire, and Rita Jeremy. *Adolescent Pregnancy and Parenting in California: A Strategic Plan for Action.* 1988. California Medical Association/California Adolescent Pregnancy Conference, Pat Murray, P.O. Box 7690, San Francisco, CA 94120-7690. 210 pp. $20.00.
Includes a great deal of information which would be helpful to other states interested in developing a statewide plan for action toward dealing with teen pregnancy and parenting.

Card, Josefina J., Editor. *Evaluating Programs Aimed at Preventing Teenage Pregnancies.* 1989. Sociometrics Corporation, 170 State Street, #260, Los Altos, CA 94022. 415/949-3282. 125 pp, $20.
Thorough and well-written guide for evaluating the results of programs intended to prevent teenage pregnancy.

Cassell, Carol, and Pamela Wilson, Editors. *Sexuality Education: A Resource Book.* 1989. Garland Press, 136 Madison Avenue, New York, NY 10016. 416 pp. $32.00.
An informative resource book about sexuality education in the family, in the schools, and in the community. Has twenty examples of model programs in each of those areas.

Children's Defense Fund (CDF) Adolescent Pregnancy Clearinghouse. Karen Pittman, Director. Children's Defense Fund, 122 C Street, N.W., Washington, DC 20001. 202/628-8787. Single issues, $4.50 unless otherwise noted. Annual subscription, $23.95.
CDF Adolescent Pregnancy Prevention Clearinghouse publishes six reports a year, each offering an in-depth examination of a single aspect of America's teen pregnancy crisis and its solution. Titles published through 1989 include:
Preventing Adolescent Pregnancy: What Schools Can do. 1986.
Welfare and Teen Pregnancy: What Do We Know, What Do We Do? 1986.
Adolescent Pregnancy: An Anatomy of a Social Problem in Search of Comprehensive Solutions. 1987.

Child Care: An Essential Service for Teen Parents. 1987.
*Declining Earnings of Young Men: Their Relation to
    Poverty, Teen Pregnancy, and Family Formation.* 1987.
*Opportunities for Prevention: Building After-School and
    Summer Programs for Young Adolescents.* 1987.
*Teens in Foster Care: Preventing Pregnancy and Building
    Self-Sufficiency.* 1987.
Child Support and Teen Parents. 1987.
Teen Pregnancy: An Advocate's Guide to the Numbers.
    1988. ($7.45)
Adolescent and Young Adult Fathers. 1988.
*What About the Boys? Teen Pregnancy Prevention
    Strategies.* 1988.
Teens and AIDS: Opportunities for Prevention. 1988.
*The Lessons of Multi-Site Initiatives: Serving High-Risk
    Youth.* 1989.
Tackling the Youth Employment Problem. 1989.
Service Opportunities for Youth. 1989.
Evaluation of Adolescent Pregnancy Programs. 1989.
    *Wonderful source of information on adolescent pregnancy
    issues, including statistics.*

Center for Population Options. **"The Public Cost of Teenage
    Childbearing."** 1988. (Updated each year.) CPO, 1012
    Fourteenth Street, N.W., Suite 1300, Washington, DC 20005.
    202/347-5700. $1.00. Workbook and computer program for
    calculating local costs of teen pregnancy, $90.
    *Reports that $19 billion was spent in 1987 for Aid to Fami-
    lies with Dependent Children, Medicaid, and Food Stamps.*

*Crises of Adolescence: Teenage Pregnancy: Impact on Adoles-
    cent Development.* Formulated by the Committee on Adoles-
    cence, Group for the Advancement of Psychiatry. 1986.
    Brunner/Mazel, Inc., 19 Union Square West, New York, NY
    10003. 104 pp. $13.95.
    *Biological, psychological, and social aspects of adolescent
    sexuality are addressed, followed by discussion of the char-
    acteristics of girls at risk for pregnancy and males who
    become fathers.*

Current Literature in Family Planning. Department of Education, Planned Parenthood Federation of America, Inc., 810 Seventh Avenue, New York, NY 10019. 212/541-7800. Subscription, $25/year.
Monthly classified list of books and articles recently received in the Katharine Dexter McCormick Library in the field of family planning, U.S.A. Other countries are included when the content of the article is considered to be of general interest.

Data Archive on Adolescent Pregnancy and Pregnancy Prevention (DAAPPP). ***Evaluating and Monitoring Programs for Pregnant and Parenting Teens.*** 170 State Street, #260, Los Altos, CA 94022. 415/949-3282. $20. Executive Summary and forms comprising the Minimum Evaluation Data Set, $3 and $8 respectively.
Monograph provides guidelines for the scientific evaluation of the impact of care programs for pregnant teens and/or teen mothers. A dBASE III program for collecting the data included in the minimum Evaluation Data Set is also available for $15.

————. ***Sourcebook of Comparison Data for Evaluating Adolescent Pregnancy and Parenting Programs.*** DAAPPP, Sociometrics Corporation. $15.
Useful for the evaluation of both care and prevention programs. Provides age and race stratified norms for females on a set of demographic, health, sex, fertility, education, and work-related variables forming the core of the Minimum Evaluation Data Set.

Flanagan, Joan. ***The Grassroots Fundraising Book: How to Raise Money in Your Community.*** 1982. Contemporary Books, Inc., 180 North Michigan, Chicago, IL 60601. 312/7782-9181. 344 pp. $11.95.
Remains one of the best overall guides for fundraising in a local community.

_____. *The Successful Volunteer Organization: Getting Started and Getting Results in Nonprofit, Charities, Grass Roots, and Community Groups.* 1981. Contemporary Books, Inc. 376 pp. $9.50.

Furstenberg, Frank F., Jr., J. Brooks-Gunn, and S. Philip Morgan. *Adolescent Mothers in Later Life.* 1987. Cambridge University Press, 510 North Avenue, New Rochelle, NY 10801. 1-800/227-0247. 204 pp. Hardcover, $27.95.
Excellent report of a scientifically valid seventeen-year study of a group of women who started having their babies as teens. Authors emphasize that health, counseling, and special education services provided to the Baltimore teenagers in the 1960s made a measurable difference in the quality of the women's lives in later years.

Healthy Mothers, Healthy Babies: The Community Connection. Revised 1986. Department of Health and Human Services, U.S. Public Health Service. 131 pp. Available free of charge from the National Maternal and Child Health Clearinghouse, 38th and R Streets, N.W., Washington, DC 20057.
A guide to community planning and organizing.

Jones, Elise F., et al. *Teenage Pregnancy in Industrialized Countries.* 1988. Yale University Press, 92A Yale Station, New Haven, CT 06520. 203/432-0964. 310 pages. Paper, $12.95; Hardcover, $35.
Compares data on reproductive behavior among adolescents in the United States and in thirty-five other developed countries, then examines in detail five countries thought to be similar culturally to the U.S.

Library and Information Network (L.I.N.K.). Planned Parenthood Federation of America, Inc., 810 Seventh Avenue, New York, NY 10019. $10 per search.
Computerized database of books, brochures, programs, curricula and audiovisual materials on all aspects of sexuality education.

Lindsay, Jeanne, and Sharon Rodine. *Teen Pregnancy Challenge, Book Two: Programs for Kids.* 1989. Morning Glory Press, 6595 San Haroldo Way, Buena Park, CA 90620. 714/828-1998. 256 pp. $14.95. Two-book set, $24.95. *Companion volume to Teen Pregnancy Challenge, Book One: Strategies for Change. Book Two focuses on adolescent pregnancy prevention and care programs.*

Lindsay, Lois. *How to Create a Teen Advisor Project: A Training Manual.* 1987. The Salvation Army Booth Memorial Center, East Bay Perinatal Council, 2794 Garden Street, Oakland, CA 94601. 415/535-5055. $5.00. *Good description of the advantages of utilizing teen advisors, and offers information on recruitment, selection, training, evaluation of training, supervision, and implementation of activities, and products of the project.*

Littell, Julia H. *Building Strong Foundations: Evaluation Strategies for Family Resource Programs.* 1986. Family Resource Coalition, 230 North Michigan Avenue, #1625. Chicago, IL 60601. 312/726-4750. 246 pp. $13.50. *A good workbook on evaluation for program providers.*

Lovick, Sharon R., and Renee Freedman Stern. *School-Based Clinics: 1988 Update.* 1988. Support Center/Center for Population Options, 5650 Kirby Drive, Suite 203, Houston, TX 77005. 703/664-7400. 20 pp., $3.00. *Highlights many aspects of school-based clinic programming. Statistics, policies, financing, and a listing of operational programs are included.*

_____, _____, Ed. *Clinic News.* Support Center/CPO, 5650 Kirby Drive, Suite 203, Houston, TX 77005. 713/664-7400. Quarterly publication, $15/year. *Reading Clinic News is a good way to keep up to date on school-based clinic information.*

Media & Values. *The Birds, the Bees and Broadcasting: What the Media Teaches Our Kids About Sex.* Spring, 1989. *Media & Values,* 1962 S. Shenandoah, Los Angeles, CA 90034. $4.00. Bulk discounts.

*Produced in collaboration with the Center for Population Options, this issue of **Media and Values** covers the impact of media sexuality by focusing on recent research in the field. Creative ways are presented for parents and leaders to initiate sexuality education around the sexual messages of prime-time television.*

Moore, Kristin A., Ph.D. **"Facts at a Glance."** Child Trends, Inc., 2100 M Street, N.W., Washington, DC 20037. Six pp. Single copy, free.
Information on teenage pregnancy and parenthood in the United States is updated annually. May be reproduced and disseminated as needed.

National Resource Center for Youth Services. **Partnerships for Youth 2000: A Program Models Manual.** 1988. NRCYS, University of Oklahoma, 125 N. Greenwood Avenue, Tulsa, OK 74120. 918/585-2986. Single copy free. May be duplicated.
Manual describes seventy-two community-level programs which are effectively addressing the problems identified by the Youth 2000 Initiative—illiteracy, school dropouts, alcohol and other substance abuse, unemployment, teen pregnancy, and violent and accidental injuries and deaths.

National Urban League. **Adolescent Male Responsibility: Pregnancy Prevention and Parenting Program: A Program Development Guide.** 1987. A report of the Adolescent Male Responsibility Project. National Urban League, 500 East 62nd Street, New York, NY 10021. 212/310-9000. Single copy free.
Includes profiles of twenty-six programs.

NOAPP Network. Quarterly newsletter. National Organization on Adolescent Pregnancy and Parenting, Box 2365, Reston, VA 22090. 16-24 pp./issue. Included with annual membership fee: $25, individual; $75, organization.
Legislation, program, research, and other topics dealing with adolescent pregnancy, parenthood, and prevention. Many resource reviews.

Options. Center for Population Options, 1012 14th Street, N.W.,
Suite 1200, Washington, DC 20005. 202/347-5700. Quarterly
publication available free of charge.
Newsletter concerned with adolescent health issues, particularly teen pregnancy prevention and AIDS education.

Pooley, Lynn E., and Julia H. Littell. *Family Resource Program
Builder: Blueprints for Designing and Operating Programs
for Parents.* 1986. Family Resource Coalition, 230 North
Michigan Avenue, #1625, Chicago, IL 60601. 312/726-4750.
246 pp. $16.00.
A good overview of the basics of program planning.

*Reaching Out: A Directory of National Organizations Related
to Maternal and Child Health.* 1989. National Maternal and
Child Health Clearinghouse, 38th and R Streets, N.W.,
Washington, DC 20057. 118 pages. Single copy free.
*Provides information on more than five hundred national
organizations which have a maternal and child health focus.
It also provides a state-by-state listing of self-help
clearinghouses.*

Resource Book. 1988. Ann M. Wilson, Director, New Jersey
Network on Adolescent Pregnancy, 73 Easton Avenue, New
Brunswick, NJ 08903. 201/932-8636.
*Beautifully edited book of data on pregnant and parenting
teens in New Jersey.*

*Risk and Responsibility: Teaching Sex Education in America's
Schools Today.* 1989. The Alan Guttmacher Institute, 111
Fifth Avenue, New York, NY 10003. 24 pp. $3.00. Bulk
discounts.
*Important research report for anyone interested in or
concerned about Family Life Education in our schools.*

Robinson, Bryan. *Teenage Fathers.* 1988. Lexington Books,
125 Spring Street, Lexington, MA 02173. 617/860-1148. 173
pages. Paper, $14.95; Hardcover, $25.00.

*Comprehensive guide to the much neglected role of the father
in teenage pregnancies. Combines numerous case studies
with important research findings and information on
programs and resources.*

Rosen, Jacqueline, Joelle Sander, and Theresa Rogers with Mary
Cannon. ***Teenage Parents and Their Families: Findings
and Guidelines from a Collaborative Effort to Promote
Family Competence.*** 1988. Bank Street College of Educa-
tion, Adolescent Family Life Collaboration, 610 West 112
Street, New York, NY 10025. 212/222-6700, x 399. 124 pp.
*A final report presenting the findings and guidelines from a
three-year family involvement demonstration project funded
by the Office of Adolescent Pregnancy Programs,
Department of Health and Human Services
(OAPP/DHHS).*

Sanders, Joelle. ***Working with Teenage Fathers: A Handbook
for Program Development.*** 1986. Bank Street College of
Education, 610 West 112th Street, New York, NY 10025.
*Describes implementation of programs for fathers. Focuses
on wide range of issues including agency politics, hiring of
male staff workers, effective recruitment strategies, core
services, and staff development.*

Schorr, Lisbeth, with news commentator Daniel Schorr. ***Within
Our Reach: Breaking the Cycle of Disadvantage.*** 1988.
Doubleday. 384 pp. $19.95.
*Based on exhaustive research, this provides insightful analy-
sis of those social policy interventions which have been successful at improving the odds for children born at risk. Early
intervention is emphasized.*

**"Sex Education: A Bibliography of Educational Materials
for Children, Adolescents, and Their Families, 1988-
1989."** American Academy of Pediatrics, 141 Northwest
Point Boulevard, P.O. Box 927, Elk Grove Village, IL
60009-0927. $20/100.

SHARE Resource Center on Teen Pregnancy Prevention.
P.O. Box 30666, Bethesda, MD 20814. 301/907-6523;
1-800/537-3788.
*Clearinghouse for data and information related to teen
pregnancy prevention which is available to program professionals as well as the general public. Database includes
current materials on all programs, statistics and curricula
from DHHS research and grants; similar information from
the state and local level; and materials from the private
sector.*

TEC Network. Funded by the Charles Stewart Mott Foundation.
For information, contact TEC Newsletter, SWRL, 4665
Lampson Avenue, Los Alamitos, CA 90720.
*Excellent newsletter concerned with adolescent pregnancy
and parenthood issues.*

"Teen Parenting: A Selected Annotated Bibliography." 1986.
Clearinghouse on Child Abuse and Neglect Information, P.O.
Box 1182, Washington, DC 20013. 18 pp.
*Lists resources from about 1980 to 1985, period generally
not covered by other references listed here.*

Teen Pregnancy Crisis: Libraries Can Help. 1988. American
Library Association, 50 East Huron Street, Chicago, IL
60611; 312/944-6780. Information packet, $12.50.
*Convenient collection of materials on teen sexuality and
pregnancy. Includes background information, resource lists,
bibliographies, program ideas.*

Teenage Pregnancy. 1988. Hot Topics Series. Center on Evalu-
ation Development, Research. Phi Delta Kappa, International
Headquarters, Eighth and Union, P.O. Box 789,
Bloomington, IN 47402-0789. $20.00.
*Twenty-nine articles dealing with many aspects of teenage
pregnancy are reprinted from such pubications as **Family
Planning Perspectives, Adolescence, Journal of Marriage
and Family.***

"Teenage Pregnancy: Developing Life Options." Association
of Junior Leagues, Inc., 660 First Avenue, New York, NY
10016-3241. Free booklet.
Nice overview of teen pregnancy issues.

**"The Facts of Love in the Library: Making Sexuality Infor-
mation Relevant and Accessible to Young People."** ALA
Video, 50 East Huron Street, Chicago, IL 60611;
312/944-6780. 20 minutes. $145.
*Developed by the American Library Association to help
librarians understand and take on their responsibility for
providing sex-related information to teenagers, and making
this information easy to locate.*

Treanor, Bill. *Barriers in Developing Comprehensive and
Effective Youth Services.* 1989. American Youth Work
Center, 1751 N Street, N.W., Suite 302, Washington, DC
20036. 202/785-0764. $10.00.
*Prepared for the W. T. Grant Foundation's Commission on
Work, Family and Citizenship by AYWC Director. Describes
the realities and demands of youth work and its management,
and offers insight into problems with funders, board members, community and staff, and other issues critical to the
operation of successful youth programs.*

Weatherley, Richard A., Sylvia B. Perlman, Michael Levine and
Lorraine V. Klerman. *Patchwork Programs: Comprehensive
Services for Pregnant and Parenting Adolescents.* 1985.
Center for Social Welfare Research, School of Social Work,
University of Washington, Seattle, WA 98195.
206/543-5640. 264 pp. $13.00.
*Compares comprehensive services for pregnant and
parenting adolescents at selected sites.*

Index

About the Authors

Jeanne Warren Lindsay, M.A., C.H.E., and Sharon Rodine, M.Ed., have worked with young people for many years. Each speaks frequently at conferences across the country.

Sharon Rodine has nearly twenty years experience in leadership positions in local, state, and national organizations focused on issues of concern to women, young people, and their families. In August, 1989, she was elected president of the National Women's Political Caucus. She has served as the executive director of the National Organization on Adolescent Pregnancy and Parenting (NOAPP) for more than five years. Prior to directing the national adolescent pregnancy network, she directed the Texas Association Concerned with Adolescent Parenthood, statewide adolescent pregnancy coalition, and served as the director of the Downtown Branch, YWCA, Houston, Texas.

Sharon and her husband, Dick, have two young sons.

Jeanne founded the Teen Mother Program in the ABC Unified School District, Cerritos, California, and continues as a consultant to the program.

She is the author of *Teens Parenting: The Challenge of Babies and Toddlers, Pregnant Too Soon: Adoption Is an Option, Adoption Awareness: A Guide for Teachers, Counselors, Nurses and Caring Others* (co-author), and five other books dealing with single parenting, teenage marriage, and adoption. She edits the *NOAPP Network,* NOAPP's quarterly newsletter.

She and Bob have been married for thirty-eight years, and have five children.

ALSO BY JEANNE LINDSAY/SHARON RODINE:

TEEN PREGNANCY CHALLENGE, Book Two:
Programs for Kids
Read abut exciting programs all along the adolescent pregnancy
prevention continuum—from primary prevention to parenting
support.

OTHER BOOKS BY JEANNE WARREN LINDSAY:

TEENS PARENTING: The Challenge of Babies and Toddlers
How to parent the first two years—with an emphasis on the special
needs of teenage parents.

PREGNANT TOO SOON: Adoption Is an Option
Advocates choice. Young women who were, by their own admission,
"pregnant too soon," tell their stories.

TEENAGE MARRIAGE: Coping with Reality
Gives teenagers a picture of the realities of marriage—a look at the
difficulties they may encounter if they say "I do" too soon.

TEENS LOOK AT MARRIAGE: Rainbows, Roles and Reality
Describes the research behind *Teenage Marriage*. Helps you understand
the culture of teenage couples.

ADOPTION AWARENESS: A Guide for Teachers, Nurses,
Counselors and Caring Others (with Catherine Monserrat)
A guide for anyone wishing to support the adoption alternative in crisis
pregnancy.

PARENTS, PREGNANT TEENS AND THE ADOPTION OPTION:
Help for Families
For all parents who feel alone and without support for themselves as
their daughter faces too-early pregnancy and the difficult adoption/
keeping decision.

DO I HAVE A DADDY? A Story About a Single-Parent Child
Picture/story book especially for children with only one parent. Includes
special ten-page section for single parent.

OPEN ADOPTION: A Caring Option
A fascinating and sensitive account of the new world of adoption. Read
about birthparents choosing adoptive parents for their baby and adoptive
parents maintaining contact with their baby's birthparents.

Please see ordering information on back of page.

MORNING GLORY PRESS
6595 San Haroldo Way, Buena Park, CA 90620
714/828-1998

Please send me the following:

Quantity	Title	Price	Total

Teen Pregnancy Challenge, Book 1: Strategies for Change

	Paper, ISBN 0930934-34-2	$14.95	_____
	Cloth, ISBN 0930934-35-0	19.95	_____

Teen Pregnancy Challenge, Book 2: Programs for Kids

	Paper, ISBN 0930934-38-5	14.95	_____
	Cloth, ISBN 0930934-39-3	19.95	_____

SPECIAL—**Teen Pregnancy Challenge—2-book set**

	Paper, ISBN 0930934-40-7	24.95	_____
	Cloth, ISBN 0930934-41-5	34.95	_____

Teenage Parents: Coping with Three-Generation Living
   Available spring, 1990

Teens Parenting: The Challenge of Babies and Toddlers

	Paper, ISBN 0930934-06-7	9.95	_____

Pregnant Too Soon: Adoption Is an Option

	Paper, ISBN 0930934-25-3	9.95	_____
	Cloth, ISBN 0930934-26-1	15.95	_____

Adoption Awareness: A Guide for Teachers, Counselors, Nurses and Caring Others

	Paper, ISBN 0930934-32-6	12.95	_____
	Cloth, ISBN 0930934-33-4	17.95	_____

Parents, Pregnant Teens and the Adoption Option

	Paper, ISBN 0930934-28-8	8.95	_____
	Cloth, ISBN 0930934-29-6	13.95	_____

Teenage Marriage: Coping with Reality

	Paper, ISBN 0930934-30-x	9.95	_____
	Cloth, ISBN 0930934-31-8	15.95	_____

Teens Look at Marriage: Rainbows, Roles and Reality		9.95	_____
Teenage Pregnancy: A New Beginning		10.00	_____
Working with Childbearing Adolescents		12.95	_____
Do I Have a Daddy? A Story About a Single-Parent Child		3.95	_____
Open Adoption: A Caring Option		9.95	_____
	TOTAL		_____

Please add postage: 1-3 bks, $2; 4+, 60¢/book. _____
California residents add 6% sales tax. _____
Ask about quantity discounts, Teacher's Guides, Study Guides.   TOTAL _____

Prepayment requested. School/library purchase orders accepted. If not satisfied, return in 15 days for refund.

NAME _____

ADDRESS _____

_____